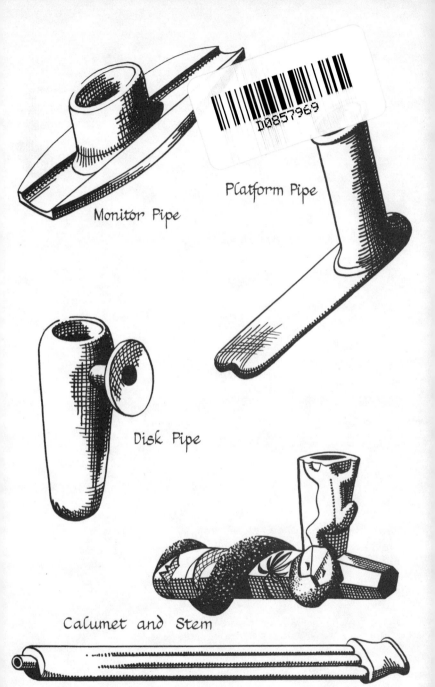

Monitor Pipe

Platform Pipe

Disk Pipe

Calumet and Stem

TOBACCO AND KENTUCKY

Metropolitan Woman's Club of Lexington
Betty Haggin Molloy
Mutual Federal Savings & Loan Association
National Industries, Inc. / Rand McNally & Company
Philip Morris, Incorporated / Mrs. Victor Sams
Shell Oil Company, Louisville
South Central Bell Telephone Company
Southern Belle Dairy Co. Inc.
Standard Oil Company (Kentucky)
Standard Printing Co., H. M. Kessler, President
State Bank & Trust Company, Richmond
Thomas Industries Inc. / Tip Top Coal Co., Inc.
Mary L. Wiss, M.D.
Younger Woman's Club of St. Matthews

Tobacco and Kentucky

W. F. AXTON

Illustrations by the Author

THE UNIVERSITY PRESS OF KENTUCKY

Research for The Kentucky Bicentennial Bookshelf
is assisted by a grant from the
National Endowment for the Humanities.
Views expressed in the Bookshelf do not
necessarily represent those of the Endowment.

ISBN: 0-8131-0207-3

Library of Congress Catalog Card Number: 74-18929

A statewide cooperative scholarly publishing agency
serving Berea College, Centre College of Kentucky,
Eastern Kentucky University, Georgetown College,
Kentucky Historical Society, Kentucky State University,
Morehead State University, Murray State University,
Northern Kentucky State College, Transylvania University,
University of Kentucky, University of Louisville, and
Western Kentucky University.

Editorial and Sales Offices: Lexington, Kentucky 40506

Contents

Illustrations follow page 132

Preface

Surely the least likely candidate to essay the first full-length history of Kentucky's tobacco, informal as this is, must be the author of the present volume, a professor of Victorian literature at the University of Louisville. Aside from an undergraduate degree in history, I have but one qualification for this task—my father, Edwin Dymond Axton, Sr., and his brother Wood were founders of what became in the 1930s the last major tobacco company owned and managed by Kentuckians, the Axton-Fisher Tobacco Company.

Thus I grew up with the rich aroma of tobacco often in my nostrils and with the lore of leaf constantly in my ears. My father was a gentle man of scholarly turn of mind, a splendid raconteur, and a great natural teacher; and at his knee I imbibed the information upon which the broad outlines of this study are based. Were he alive today, he would be a hundred years old; and he would have been the most appropriate person to have written this book. Acting as his surrogate, I dedicate this volume to his memory, in the sure and certain knowledge that, in his great rocking chair up yonder, he is reading these pages and, what is more, fulminating against the errors committed by that ignorant young puppy, their author.

These sentimental associations extend to include in their embrace an industrial giant, Philip Morris Incorporated, which purchased Axton-Fisher over a generation ago and now operates its much-expanded plant in Louisville with great success. In recognition of these bonds, Philip Morris generously agreed to underwrite the bulk of the publication costs of this volume, after the manuscript was completed and without asking to exercise any editorial control over its contents. Such a gratifying gesture in token of a shared sense of historical continuity is all the more poignant because of my longstanding friendship with James C. Bowling, a senior officer of Philip Morris, an alumnus of the University of Louisville, and the younger brother of an old wartime comrade, Van Dorn Bowling, Jr. It does seem to be a small world after all, and sometimes, as on this occasion, a reassuringly human one.

It is quite impossible to acknowledge all the other debts I owe to the dozens of colleagues, friends, and interested citizens who have assisted me in the preparation of this text; but special thanks belong to my research assistants, Ivol Parker and Katherine Auerbach; to Anne Owen and Alice Cole, who typed the manuscript from my longhand sheafs of legal cap; and to the librarians of a half-dozen different collections at the University of Louisville, who were unfailingly generous with their help.

Notable extracurricular assistance came from the following: my brother, Edwin Dymond Axton, Jr., an inexhaustible source of documents, oral history, and martinis; "Kenny" Kremer, proprietor of Kremer's Smoke Shoppe, an indispensable Louisville institution, and philosopher extraordinaire to tobacco users; two trusting souls who lent me, sight unseen, important original documents, Robert Hobson, statistician for the Tennessee Crop Reporting Service, and John E. Gallaher, Greater Lexington Chamber of Commerce; and C. R. Corum, who let me use his manuscript article "Tobacco, the Winged Pipe, and the Sioux Religion."

A unique accolade belongs to my wife, Anne Millard Axton, who had to listen to me talk these pages through.

1

"Soul-Consoling Smoke": The First 10,000 Years

A PRESIDING IRONY in the history of the place we recent settlers call Kentucky is that, aside from a pamphlet or two and a few journal articles here and there, the story of tobacco, the Commonwealth's most important crop and, next to bourbon whisky, its best-known manufactured product, has not been told until now. Indeed, successive historians from Humphrey Marshall down to the present have hardly given more than passing attention to the starring role played by the various strains of Burley leaf and the products made from them in the economic and social life of this state, although everyone acknowledges their importance.

No less ironic is that most histories of Kentucky largely deal with only the recent past, that period beginning with the arrival of European explorers and settlers in the last half of the eighteenth century, as though "history" means "what happens to white people." And yet we know from anthropologists and archeologists that Kentucky's rich meadows and forests were inhabited for many thousands of years before the invasion of Europeans by a succession of fascinating and gifted peoples, almost all of whom, among their other accomplishments, were skillful agriculturalists who first gathered and then cultivated tobacco, developed the various methods of processing and using it, and bequeathed the results of this high technology to the Caucasians who displaced them.

Therefore, a history of tobacco in Kentucky must begin with the original settlers, the Paleoindians and their successors the Amerindians. Along with corn, peanuts, the tomato, and the "Irish" potato, tobacco is a gift from the peoples of the New World to the Old, some of whom by 1492 had achieved a higher level of civilization—at least in agriculture—than that of Western Europe, and who were inveterate users of tobacco.

When these peoples came to the Americas, where they came from, even how they got here, is still not known with any certainty. We assume that the first settlers originated somewhere in Asia and traveled to this continent over the Aleutian land bridge created when the level of the seas was lowered by the moisture captured in the enormous polar ice cap and glacial fields during the last great glaciation. This migration may have begun as early as 38,000 years ago, certainly no later than 13,000 years ago.

Who these peoples may have been is equally obscure, for many are now known only by the sites where their traces have been unearthed. Sandia man, Clovis man, the llano people (who had spread coast-to-coast by 12,000–14,000 years ago and may very well have inhabited Kentucky), Folsom man, Plainview man, and Plano man—these were big-game hunters. They stalked the great and now-extinct animals that grazed and browsed in Kentucky then: the woolly mammoths, giant tapirs and sloths, big-horned bisons, early horses (Eohippus), camels, giant armadillos, and the Columbian mammoths, the last of which were exterminated by 5500 B.C. They hunted these mighty creatures collectively, often stampeding an entire herd over a cliff in order to butcher a few carcasses for meat, pelts, sinews, bone, and horn, and generally preying upon the young. Whatever the reasons may have been for the extinction of these species, the hunting methods of our Paleoindian predecessors played an important part.[1]

But long before the final end of the Paleoindians' big-game hunting culture, preadaptive cultures were emerging all over the Americas which were well fitted to a more sedentary and localized existence based on small game, fish, birds, berries, roots, fruit, and seeds, and which slowly evolved the paraphernalia of settled, civilized life: snares and fish spears, darts, baskets, milling stones, and a diet of wild meat supplemented by gathered vegetation. Flint tools and weapons were already being beautifully worked; and by 4000 B.C. the Eastern Archaic peoples of our region were fashioning sophisticated implements of copper, horn, bone, flint, and many other materials, and living on a diverse diet of wild game and fowl, fish, shellfish, and crustaceans, wild plants, roots, nuts, seeds, and grains, some of which were ground into meal. In short, the diet of these peoples was similar to that of the Eastern Woodland Indians first encountered by European explorers. These Indians were also smoking tobacco for a variety of ritual, social, and diplomatic purposes as well as for personal pleasure. This practice may have been an ancient one among the natives, for early stone pipes have been carbon-dated as early as 5,000 years ago, or about 3000 B.C.; and this fact suggests that the use of tobacco may belong to the very first agricultural stages of civilization in the New World.

1. A further irony emerges: Eohippus, whose origins lay in the Western Hemisphere, apparently escaped into Asia by the Aleutian land bridge before its extinction on this continent. After further evolution and domestication in Eurasia, he returned to the Americas with the Spanish as the modern horse. Taken up by western settlers and the Plains Indians as the pinto pony, the horse played a crucial role in the near-extinction of the American bison, the last survivor of the great paleolithic creatures, during the nineteenth century.

Agricultural development of our continent is still obscure as compared to fairly reliable guesses about the date and location of the beginnings of settled agricultural life in the Old World. There, in the Tigris-Euphrates Valley about 9000 B.C., an agriculture based on the relatively easily domesticated wheat, barley, and rye was begun. Over here, caves in the Tehuaccán Valley south of Mexico City have revealed traces of human habitation dating back to 10,000 B.C. By some time between 7000 and 5000 B.C. both wild and domesticated plants were being used to supplement game and other foods; and the first wild maize (corn with ears the size of a thumbnail) seems to have been eaten. By about 3500 B.C. agriculture accounted for a third of the total food supply and permanent settlement had been established; and 2,000 years later a complex village life was in full flower, including a settled agriculture, pottery, a social structure with a ritualized religion, and other trappings of civilization.

During the thousands of years that ensued until the arrival of the Spanish conquistadores, a remarkably advanced civilization evolved on an agricultural base more diverse and sophisticated than Europe had ever known. The technical skill required to domesticate maize into corn is greater than that needed to make viable crops of wheat, barley, and rye; and, together with squash, potatoes, tomatoes, beans, yams, and with such medicines as quinine, ipecac, and cascara, the agriculture of the Western Hemisphere was very rich and varied. It was the natives of the Americas who, for example, discovered the process of extracting the poison from the manioc root in order to make tapioca, an important source of protein still used today. And these same peoples also learned the uses of another toxic plant, tobacco, and domesticated it for a host of purposes.

Some years ago it was argued that tobacco was an importation of the Old World into the New, chiefly on the

4

evidence of prehistoric pipes excavated at a number of sites bordering the Mediterranean Sea and inland in Asia Minor. These pipes, however, are now thought to have been employed for the consumption of cannabis (marijuana) and other herbs, plants, and substances (notably dried cow dung) with a variety of medicinal, sacramental, or narcotic functions. Fumigation with, or the inhalation of, the smoke of various substances has been a sacred, healing, or pleasurable practice of homo sapiens since time immemorial. The smoke of such substances has long been known or supposed to alter consciousness, induce trance, stupefaction, or visions, to purify, heal, or tranquilize. Moreover, the smoke of pungent herbs and plants appeared to make visible (if intangible) the divine spirit, and, by being inhaled, seemed capable of incorporating that spirit with the human frame, thereby providing an avenue of communion with the deity. Smoke as incense might also serve as an offering to the gods. If the smoke possessed some drug or narcotic property that acted upon the mind of the inhalant, then the supernatural qualities of fumigation or inhalation seemed doubly confirmed. As with cannabis and opium, so with tobacco and many other substances.

It is now believed that tobacco is almost certainly a native American plant, but not native to Canada or to the eastern two-thirds of the Americas, including Kentucky. The wild tobaccos from which domesticated strains were derived—botanists have counted about sixty varieties of them—were native to the slopes of the great mountainous spine that runs along the extreme western edge of our continent. Although in what is now the United States wild tobaccos grew only along the western, or Pacific, side of the Rockies, in Central and South America the plant grew more widely on either side of the Andes and well south of Peru and Ecuador. Only two strains of wild tobaccos are important to our story, *Nicotiana rusticum*, and *Nicotiana tabacum*.[2] The former, a small-leafed, harsh-smoking variety, appears to have spread northward from Mexico up the Pacific coast and, perhaps shortcutting through the tribes of the Southwest, out into the great basin, and so on east to the Atlantic and north into Canada. It was this tobacco that the Indians were smoking in their "Calumets" (right-angled stone elbow pipes) when the English and French explorers and settlers penetrated the Great Lakes. *N. tabacum* seems to have originated on the eastern Andean piedmont of Ecuador and Peru, spread eastward into the Amazon basin, and was then carried northward by the migrations of the Arawak and Tupi-Guarani peoples as far as Cuba, Venezuela, and the isthmus of Panama, where it met and mingled with *N. rustica*. *N. tabacum*, however, became the foundation stock of almost all the tobaccos presently grown in the United States for commercial purposes, for it was a milder, larger-leafed, richer-tasting hybrid, with as yet unrealized potentialities for evolution. Its superiority, moreover, seems to have been recognized as soon as it was established as a domesticated strain, for wherever it became known and seeds were available, *N. tabacum* was adopted for the pleasurable uses of tobacco at least. For religious purposes, on the other hand, other native strains of tobacco like *N. rusticum* continued in use among Indians, even alongside *N. tabacum*, right down to the present.

Although we cannot date with any certainty the dis-

2. *Nicotiana*, the general botanical name for all tobaccos, memorializes Jean Nicot, the French physician and scientist who introduced tobacco (probably *N. rusticum*) into France in 1560, naming it the "Queen's Herb" in honor of Catherine de Medici, and making many fabulous medicinal claims for it. The term nicotine derives from the same source. Modern tobacco, *N. tabacum*, was probably introduced into France from Brazil three years earlier by Jean Andre Thevet, a Huguenot, now almost forgotten.

covery of tobacco, the beginning of its various uses, medicinal, religious, narcotic, or pleasurable, nor even its initial domestication, it must have been very ancient indeed and was probably first gathered in a wild state. Traces of tobacco use among ancient peoples of America would be hard to come by before the development of smoking implements such as stone pipes, which have been discovered by modern archeologists and paleontologists in camping sites and burial grounds dating back many thousands of years, since the plant itself, or its leaves, would soon disintegrate and disappear, and unlike many other ancient plants which can be readily identified by their seeds, cobs, or pods, the seeds of the tobacco plant are almost invisible. The great Swedish botanist of the eighteenth century, Linnaeus, counted 40,320 seeds in a single pod of *N. tabacum* and estimated that a healthy plant has a potential production of 1 million seeds. Nowadays it is estimated that an ounce will contain between 300,000 and 400,000 seeds.

Nevertheless, there is much indirect evidence about the scope and nature of the early history of tobacco in its presumed birthplace, Central and South America. The most intriguing fragment is a carved bas-relief unearthed in the ruins of a Mayan temple, the foundation of which can be dated by calendar collation quite precisely at March 12, A.D. 432. Familiarly called "The Old Man of Palenque" after the location of its site on the Yucatan Peninsula, the stone depicts a Mayan priest or shaman clad in the skin of a jaguar. He is blowing smoke out of the lighted end of a long tube held in his mouth, a "chamal" or cigar or cane tube holding leaf (most probably the latter). The Priest of Palenque appears not to be smoking, as we understand the term, but blowing the smoke out as a fumigant or incense. From a variety of other sources we believe that the substance producing the smoke was tobacco, perhaps mixed with other materials; for from the beginning leaf has been adulterated by a great number of other substances—and

7

still is. Indeed, among the Maya tobacco was a sacred plant employed as a ritual offering to the Jaguar-Sun-God in hopes that he would bring rain to the crops during the dry season.

As to many other peoples of the Americas, tobacco was intimately associated with their gods not only in their religious observances but also in their curative or healing procedures, all of which were connected in one way or another with their religion. The peoples of the Americas were always remarkably inventive in adapting plants to their uses. By the time of the arrival of the European explorers in the late fifteenth century, for example, the peoples of North America, many of whom roamed the woodlands, canebrakes, and savannahs of Kentucky, were regularly employing some 275 species of plants for medicinal purposes, 130 for food, 31 as charms, 27 for smoking, 25 as dyes, 18 as beverages and for flavorings, and 52 others for various purposes: a total of 558. And, compared to the cultures of Central and South America, these were relatively primitive peoples.

Among the literally thousands of plants used by the original settlers of this hemisphere, tobacco played a prominent role, particularly in medicine. Besides serving as a general purifying agent designed to drive away evil spirits, the smoke of burning tobacco was used to cure colic, overweight, and gastric and bronchial difficulties, even to tranquilize. With fat and salt, tobacco powder was employed in what must have been a formidable suppository. It was taken internally as a purgative and cure for worms. Chewed, it was thought to aid toothache; and spat out afterwards it was employed as a disinfectant for cuts and bruises (it still is, among southern farm folk), as an emollient for snake, spider, and insect bites, and as a poultice for chest colds, boils, internal infections, and inflammations (again, it still is so employed). Mixed with lard, tobacco continues to be a specific against body lice in southern rural districts, and at one time it was used among native Americans as a toothpaste and even a painkiller.

By the time of the first Spanish and Portuguese explorers of the New World, tobacco seems to have been used widely throughout the Caribbean as an addictive narcotic, often in combination with, or as a substitute for, more powerful drugs. Tobacco was sometimes reduced to a floury powder and mixed with pulverized shells of fresh-water or salt-water mollusks. The resulting compound was rolled into pills and carried by the Indians to be eaten as an appetite suppressant much in the manner that betel nuts are still employed in some places. Along with many other more powerful narcotic substances—cocaine, cohoba, cogiado (the latter two derivatives of the seed of the powerfully psychoactive Piptadenia peregrina), with which tobacco was often mixed (and by early European observers often confused)—tobacco was commonly ground into snuff and inhaled. The device employed to inhale this snuff, a Y-shaped forked tube designed to fit the nostrils on one end with a single inhaling orifice on the other, was called a "tobago," from which the name of "tobacco" was derived in consequence of the common error in translation of confusing the instrument with the thing used by the instrument.

However that may be, the earliest writers about the New World, like Oviedo (1535), Las Casas (1552), Bernaz Diaz del Castillo (1558), Monardes (1571), and Benzoni (1565), observed tobacco being used, alone or with other substances, for ceremonial, medicinal, and pleasurable purposes in every form now enjoyed by modern men and women. Its leaves were put into the mouth and chewed, or, in the case of the broad-leafed *N. tabacum* which flourished on Hispaniola (Cuba), rolled into cigars and smoked.[3] The practice of inhaling the smoke

3. The term cigar derives from the Spanish word *cigarra,* the name given to the large balm-cricket that the rolled leaves

for its narcotic effect seems to have been well known among the natives, because the astonished Spaniards observed the Indians "drinking" the smoke to induce, variously, intoxication, trance, even unconsciousness. Crumbled, tobacco was packed in tubes of cane, reed, or bamboo, or wrapped in cornhusks, and smoked very much like modern cigarettes. Perhaps out of this practice evolved the age-old smoking device of the pipe, made out of either stone or pottery, which was initially a hollowed tube and only later evolved into the form most familiar to us: an upright bowl connected to a hollow stem and mouthpiece. Tobacco was also made into a narcotic drink which, taken under conditions of isolation and fasting for mystical or prophetic purposes, produced hallucinations or visions that had a central place in the religions of many peoples of the Americas. Tobacco thus joins that select group of hallucinogenic or narcotic substances upon which the mystic or ecstatic religions of so many native American peoples were based. Bequeathed to Europeans and used by them for very different and not so lofty purposes, they have had a profound effect on the manners and morals of Western man: these include datura (jimsonweed), northern holly, southern holly (maté), peyote (cactus), mushrooms, pulque, coca (whence cocaine, Sherlock Holmes's comforter), and cohoba (the narcotic snuff of the Haitians).

Nearly all the peoples of America believed in the divine origin of tobacco and in its sacred visionary or ecstatic properties; it was held by them in great veneration. On October 14, 1492, tobacco was first seen by Columbus himself near San Salvador Island (now Watling Island, one of the Lesser Bahamas), when a hand of its leaves was offered to him as a gift by a reverent native. The last Inca was named Saire Tupac, which may

---

of early cigars somewhat resembled. "Cigarette" is of course a French diminutive form of "cigar."

be loosely translated "Tobacco Royal"; "Saire" meant tobacco (*N. tabacum*), either pure or mixed with the more narcotic powder prepared from the seeds of Piptadenia peregrina and used as a snuff. Among the Maya, there were two words for tobacco: "kutz," meaning to beguile or deceive, and referring to the tobacco plant; and "mai," meaning to count by twenties as well as referring to the powdered tobacco prepared for incense or for smoking. This latter association between tobacco and numbers suggests their occult relationship. Gourds of tobacco were carried by Aztec warriors, hunters, and gods, apparently because of its magical properties; and Bernal Diaz del Castillo reported that Montezuma II smoked tobacco at a great banquet with Cortez in 1519.

In the northeastern part of what is now the United States, smoking of tobacco in stone pipes was very ancient indeed among the Algonkin peoples, and tobacco enjoyed the same wide distribution and central role in the visionary exercises, medicine, and religious ceremonies that it had in Central and South America. What makes these peoples' use of tobacco so interesting to us now are their concentration on the use of tobacco in one dominant form—smoked, and in a pipe of stone or similar material—the antiquity of this practice, and the extravagant lengths to which they apparently had to go to maintain the practice.

The story begins some 3,500–4,000 years ago, when the Eastern Archaic Culture began to give way to what is now called the Woodland Culture, which by 500 B.C. was well established. These peoples were builders of great mounds, some for burial, others for defensive purposes, still others for ceremonial and religious functions; and from the bottom forms of the mound cultures from the Mississippi River Valley and California north and east to Ontario—presumably the earliest laid down—tubular stone and clay pipes have been retrieved which were once used for smoking *N. rusticum* (see endpaper).

The Adena Culture, encompassing southern Ohio, northern Kentucky, and northwestern West Virginia, was a rich culture of huge burial mound complexes in which important personages were buried in the midst of sumptuous grave offerings and the murdered bodies of retainers. A politically and socially complex and populous culture, the Adena people produced particularly beautiful pottery with gorgeous and elaborate ornamentation; and yet they were largely a hunting and gathering culture in which agriculture did not have a major influence. On top of this culture and centered on its geographical area, but ranging out as far as Minnesota, New York, Florida, and Louisiana, the Hopewell Culture was superimposed. It was actually not a "culture" at all in the technical sense of the term, but a collection of many different societies with their own customs, institutions, and autonomy; but they were linked by a common cult of the dead and the economic bonds that cult generated in grave goods and in the extensive trade required to serve it. Copper was brought in from Lake Superior, mica from the Appalachians, obsidian (sometimes used for pipes) from the Rocky Mountains, alligator teeth and conch shells from the Gulf Coast, and pipestone from Wisconsin and Minnesota.

With the entrance of pipestone, tobacco emerges for us as an important element in an evolving native civilization based on a settled agricultural economy and village life, together with the technology that these institutions generated. Their technology was considerable, sufficient indeed to sustain an agriculture employing flint and stone tools, grinding implements for flour, meal, and pulverizing generally, devices to make yarn and thread and to weave cloth, and instruments to work stone, metal, and other hard substances. In the case of pipestone,[4] a reddish or flecked granitic stone which

4. Properly, pipestone is called Catlinite, after George Catlin, the nineteenth-century painter and historian of the Plains Indians, who investigated the pipestone quarries.

seems to have been the almost universal material for the manufacture of ceremonial pipes by the Indians and their predecessors, the very quarry in southwestern Minnesota was believed in modern times to have been the sacred birthplace of the natives, the reddish stone a monument to the color of their ancestors' flesh. In consequence they agreed that the great quarry near Pipestone, Minnesota, should be a reservation to which all Indian tribes might have free and equal access for quarrying the rough stone "blanks" that were carried back to native villages, then beautifully carved and polished, hollowed out for bowl and stem, and put into ritual smoking service. Well before the time of Jesus, for example, the Adena people were working pipestone into small cylindrical and "elbow" pipes; and the peoples of the sophisticated Hopewell Culture shaped plain platform pipes out of Catlinite and much more elaborate and beautiful platform pipes carved to represent magnificently stylized animals, birds, reptiles, even fish—for what purpose, we do not certainly know (see endpaper).

From the pipes found in burial mounds a number of hypotheses have been induced suggesting an important role for them in the ruling, priestly, or wealthy class structure of Hopewell society. Wherever pipes turn up in excavations, they appear to be associated with important personages, like the large bird pipe found on the old Peter Farm on Newtown Pike, near Lexington (see title page). By the same token, tobacco cultivation among these early inhabitants of Kentucky is as problematical as its use, for we do not know when *N. rusticum* was first grown in this region as an imported domesticated plant along with, say, maize. About the latter we are rather better informed by way of indirect evidence, such as mortars and pestles, grinding stones and millstones, hominy holes in rock, traces of corn cob, and the like; but about tobacco the surviving evidence is obscure indeed. Although we know from the evidence of stone pipes that tobacco was smoked in Kentucky as early as four or five thousand years ago, we cannot be sure how long tobacco has been cultivated on this land. The conservative view has held that tobacco was undertaken as a cultivated plant in Kentucky only fairly recently, some several generations before the arrival of Europeans. On the other hand, the aborigines encountered by English and French explorers were generally less advanced than their predecessors, if not less fierce, for even the early Cave and Cliff Dwellers of Central and Eastern Kentucky were agriculturalists who cultivated crops extensively, including corn, and who also possessed leaf tobacco. But the question is, does the presence of tobacco leaves mean that they grew their own or that they obtained them in trade, presumably with the tribes of the Southwest? My own opinion is that tobacco was grown as a domesticated crop in Kentucky from a very early date, perhaps as early as the Hopewell peoples.

However that may be, by A.D. 500 the Hopewell Culture was in decline in our region, as unrest, warfare, and raiding from the north and east spread across and inundated this, perhaps the finest culture of North America before the stage reached by the European colonists. But as the great burial mound complexes of these peoples retreated up to hilltops, where they became defensive fortifications rather than ceremonial centers, the Hopewell peoples were supplanted by another culture of splendid achievements, this time located on the streams that served the Ohio and Mississippi rivers in the southeastern part of what is now the United States.

This new culture, which extended from Ohio to Louisiana, and from Eastern Tennessee to Arkansas, is now called the Mound Builders' Culture, although we usually associate the Adena or Hopewell peoples with this term. Perhaps it is simpler to call these peoples the Mississippian Culture, since the mounds they built were not for purposes of burial or defense, but were pyramidal mounds, sometimes of almost Egyptian or Aztec monumentality, which served as the sites of temples for the reigning deities and for the lodges of the chiefs, who thought themselves their gods' representatives on earth—nay, their embodiments. By A.D. 1300 the culture of the Mississippians rivaled that of the Hopewell peoples in splendor and sophistication. The great urban complex at Cahokia, Illinois, just across the river from Saint Louis, was six miles long and could boast of more than eighty-five mounds dedicated to chiefs and gods, the greatest of which was one hundred feet high and covered sixteen acres at its base. The magnitude of organized human labor required to erect such an edifice suggests a monolithic social and political structure like that of the Egyptians in the time of the great pharaohs. It took its stamp as a culture from influences derived both from the peoples of Mexico and from the Adena and Hopewell civilizations, all of whom were agriculturalists and builders of mounds. Their cultural sophistication and complexity rested squarely on a base of Indian corn or maize, and tobacco played a prominent role in ritual life.

More important, the Mississippian Culture was the immediate antecedent of the powerful chiefdoms of the southeastern United States (some of whom met—and signally defeated—Desoto): the Natchez, Cherokee (southeastern Tennessee), Shawnee (northern Tennessee), Choctaw (southern Mississippi and Alabama), Chickasaw (northern Mississippi), Powhatan, Pamlico, and Tuscarora (eastern Virginia and North Carolina), and other tribes extending as far west as East Texas, Arkansas, and Louisiana, and as far east and south as Florida, the Bahamas, Cuba, and Jamaica. Like the Mississippians, these chiefdoms were monolithic cultures dedicated to sun worship; and the chief was commonly identified as the Great Sun, whose death required the ritual killing and burial with him of his wives, retainers, and guards. Before the sacrificial victims were killed, they were administered a pill of pulverized tobacco by a shaman of the tribe which caused them to lose consciousness, after which the ritual garroting took place.

These were the peoples encountered by the first settlers of Virginia, Maryland, and the Carolinas early in the seventeenth century and again by the pioneers who entered Kentucky more than a century and a half later.[5] Everywhere in Kentucky were traces of the great native cultures which had preceded the Europeans' occupation of Kentucky's verdant forests and meadowlands, not only in the impressive mound complexes but in the many survivals of the Indians' and Paleoindians' tobacco cults. Tubular pipes of sandstone and slate, often decorated with enigmatic pictographs engraved on their sides and resembling the instrument employed in the Yucatan by the "Old Man of Palenque," were found all over Kentucky, in spite of what must be their great antiquity. This was perhaps the oldest kind of pipe employed in the Western Hemisphere, and one that must have worked its way north and east out of Mexico and the Southwest, along with the herb it is designed to serve, at a very early date (see endpaper). Quite large, very skillfully carved and polished bird and animal pipes weighing several pounds and apparently designed to be smoked by several persons simultaneously, have been discovered all over the state—near Morehead in the south, near Lexington in Central Kentucky, and near Paint Lick in the northeast. "Monitor" pipes (so named because of their resemblance in profile to the Civil War ironclad battleship) have been occasionally unearthed in Kentucky, although they appear to belong to prehistoric peoples who inhabited the Great Lakes region; even a rare Micmac pipe or two, like the "Monitors" most likely an accident of trade or travel, has turned up, in testimony to the extensive Amerindian system of cul-

5. John Finley, an early explorer of Kentucky, found *N. rusticum* being cultivated by a tribe of Shawnees encamped near what is now Spring Station in 1752.

tural and commercial interchange that seems to have gone on all over North America from the earliest days (see endpaper).[6]

A fascinating design solution to the problems of smoking ground tobacco in a stone pipe is to be found in the many "disk" pipes uncovered in Kentucky. In these, the long stone bowl is only partially hollowed out to receive the tobacco, and the shank was used to hold it, while the disk was put against the lips of the smoker and the smoke inhaled through the shortest of stems. Often the bowls were richly ornamented with pictographs of animals, like a notable alligator, or even two warriors in combat. A particularly fine example made of Catlinite was found in Bourbon County (see endpaper).

The "double conoidal" pipe appears to be a particularly ancient form that is very common in Kentucky. This type is so called because both the bowl and stem holes were drilled out by a cone-shaped bit. Curiously, such pipes were often rather crudely carved to resemble faces—for what purpose we do not know—and, while they have been uncovered in mounds and gravesites, they are often ploughed up in open fields which have no connection with any prehistoric settlement. Franklin County has been the location of many fine specimens (see endpaper).

"Ovoid" pipes are associated with the venerable

6. This is perhaps not so surprising in the light of modern estimates that prehistoric North America may have been much more thickly populated than had been thought—perhaps as many as ten to twelve million people north of the Rio Grande River. These figures go far to explain the role played by the Paleoindians in the extermination of so many creatures between six and ten thousand years ago. By 1850 the Indian population of the continental United States had dwindled to about 250,000, as a result of disease, privation, and systematic extermination by whites. Today, on the other hand, there are about 800,000 Indians in North America.

burial-mound-building peoples of the Fort Ancient Culture, where these small, virtually undecorated, roundish stone pipes are often found with vase-shaped and diminutive elbow pipes—some with the ashes still in them and still smelling strongly of what pipe smokers today would call the "gummy heel" of old, smoked tobacco (see endpaper).

"Totem" pipes have been found whose origin and use are not well understood. They are called totem pipes because they were carved to represent figures of birds, fish, and wild animals native to the woods and streams of the United States, human faces, frogs, the hooves of deer, and various other objects; but they are much smaller than the heavy animal and bird pipes of the southern Indian peoples. We suppose that these effigies represent some totem or symbol of private, clan, or tribal significance, but their meaning remains elusive (see endpaper).

The prehistoric peoples of the Southeast were the great potters of North America, especially those who dwelt along the Kentucky, Tennessee, and Cumberland River valleys and farther south, such as the River People of Western Kentucky and the Cherokee and Pre-Cherokee peoples. They developed a kind of heat-resistant tempered "stone-ware," using clay mixed with the lime extracted from shells, which was employed for a wide variety of practical purposes in cooking pots, bowls and cups, water bottles, beads and ornaments, urns and vessels—and, notably, in pipes, often richly decorated with elegantly stylized animal motifs (see endpaper).

The scarcity in Kentucky of the only sort of Amerindian smoking device most of us are familiar with—the great stone Calumet or peace pipe that is still smoked ceremonially by the remnants on the Plains of these once mighty and populous nations—is explained by the lack of permanent Indian settlements in Kentucky in relatively modern times. In the culture of these peoples tobacco was a vitally important crop; and, with the great stone Calumet, the large upright elbow pipe, and its ornately carved and symbolically decorated wooden stem (which was more sacred even than the bowl), it played a central role in their religious life. Indeed, the smoking of tobacco in the Calumet by a chief, priest, or shaman constituted a ritual that was the very cornerstone of Amerindian religion. And tobacco occupied a no less prominent place in their medicine.

"Calumets" [7] were first encountered by French missionaries in the upper Mississippi River well after Jacques Cartier's and Henry Hudson's expeditions early in the sixteenth century, neither of whom mentions any instrument resembling the great stone ceremonial pipes of the latter days, although they noticed the existence of tobacco and its use by the natives. This suggests that the Calumet may have been a fairly late development in the tobacco cultus of the Eastern Woodland peoples, perhaps well after the arrival of Europeans, and perhaps, like tobacco itself, an importation from the West. On the other hand, pipestone tobacco pipes were carved and polished in a highly sophisticated manner and in a bewildering variety of different styles and shapes by a succession of peoples of North America for many centuries before Columbus, so that the great Calumet may simply be another permutation of a well established native tradition by another people.

Nevertheless we should not underestimate the significance of the "Calumet cult" when it appeared, for the new pipe shape was the visible sign of a profound spiritual transformation that swept through the peoples of

7. The term is a corruption of "chalumeau," the French word for reed, itself probably a translation of an Indian word which referred not to the unimportant bowl of the pipe but to the sacred stem. Another linguistic mix-up!

the eastern woodlands coincidental with the ritual use of tobacco. Apparently an outgrowth of a much earlier practice of casting tobacco leaves on a ritual fire as an incense offering to the gods or as a purifying medium (some eastern peoples continued this practice, and never adopted the Calumet or the habit of smoking), the inhalation of the smoke created a state of mind in which the celebrant felt that he had found favor in the eyes of his deity, and thence the long evolution of the pipe we have already traced in North America. However, smoking forged a new pattern after the potters and corn-raisers flourished in the Eastern United States and the great stone elbow pipe emerged as the principal cult object next to the wooden stem. The Calumet thereby became an altar, albeit a portable one, for burnt offerings of tobacco incense to the gods. Tobacco itself became a sacred plant, the mythical gift of one great spirit or another to the legendary founder of the tribe or people, the burning of which found favor with the gods and propitiated evil spirits. In some tribes, indeed, tobacco was so sacred that even its cultivation—much less its use—was forbidden to women; and the men oversaw the crop, its curing, and its preparation for ceremonial use. Among such tribes (usually those in arid western regions where cultivation of tobacco was difficult in the best of times and a crop sufficient for a year's use by the shamans always uncertain), smoking tobacco for pleasure seems to have been unknown. But many of the eastern tribes, who roamed Kentucky with a plentiful supply of *N. rusticum* back in their home villages, smoked for both ceremonial purposes and personal pleasure, men and women alike, although of course the sacred Calumet was never used just to light up for a quiet drag after a hard day in the council lodge. Many individuals carried pouches or gourds of tobacco around their necks when on the trail, just as the Aztecs had.

Tobacco smoked in the Calumet was much venerated

for other reasons. Tipi pictographs of Plains Indians such as the Sioux dating from sometime after the introduction of the horse around 1770 have suggested to students a puberty rite for young braves, in which a mystical winged pipe may have been the central symbol in a psychedelic ritual involving visions produced by inhaling tobacco smoke. No doubt ritual starvation and deprivation of normal stimuli played an equal part with tobacco in producing this visionary communication with the spirit world. Then as now, inhaling tobacco smoke from the sacred Calumet and stem induced trance, divination, prophecy, and hallucination among the priests and shamans of many tribes, who associated their "medicine" pipes with a godlike power which watched over the welfare of the people.

Moreover, the inhaled smoke of tobacco was thought to possess "soul-consoling" properties which the Amerindians believed to have been sent to mankind as a pledge of their protection and beneficence by the powers who control life. It may have been this concept which has prompted the quite erroneous notion that the great Calumet was a "peace pipe." It was certainly such an association of ideas among the natives of North America that endowed inhalation of tobacco smoke with the symbolic value of brotherhood—nay more, that made participation in the smoking ritual a charm that compelled brotherhood, reinforced as it was by powerful religious connotations. To share with another this sacred smoke was to participate in the divine wisdom and goodness which unifies all people, of which friendship is but one manifestation.

There is more to this matter, for the substance smoked in their Calumets by the North American aborigines was probably not pure *N. rusticum* but a blend of many materials, some narcotic, hallucinogenic, or psychoactive and some not, of which tobacco may not have accounted for more than a third. *N. rusticum* is a stridently harsh tobacco and, to become even remotely palatable, it needs to be mixed with other substances of a more ingratiating taste when burned, some of which contain different versions of the alkaloids that carry the toxic and psychoactive elements of tobacco. Thus the natives who trod the soil of what we now call Kentucky are known to have employed from earliest times a host of adulterants to sweeten their smoke—just as we do now. Various barks, of willow, cherry, laurel, ironwood, poplar, cottonwood, birch, dogwood, jimson weed (a variety of datura with well-known psychoactive properties), and others were so employed. Leaves of other plants, bushes, and trees were also used, notably laurel, sumac, manzanita (in the West), squawbush, maple bush, and bearberry (also psychoactive), even mullein. Other substances such as roots and gums have been called into service as well, the most famous being the liquidambar of the sweetgum which Montezuma so much enjoyed. So general was this practice among the Amerindians that one of their most widely used names for the stuff they smoked was Kinnikinnick, meaning "that which is mixed." Nor may these native blends be dismissed by modern smokers, for the few whites who have been allowed to participate in Calumet ceremonials testify to the mild and aromatic flavor of the mixtures smoked therein.

One matter is certain: native smoking compounds launched the craze for tobacco in all its forms that swept round the world during the sixteenth and seventeenth centuries and established its present preeminence as the most widely used addictive drug on this planet. Although it was the mellower strain of *N. tabacum,* introduced into Europe from the Caribbean and later cultivated commercially in colonial Virginia, that found worldwide acceptance for smoking purposes and was even much sought after by Amerindians from white traders, this leaf was limited by natives to pleasure smoking, and Kinnikinnick was reserved exclusively for ceremonial occasions. This distinction remains in force today among those surviving Indians who still practice the Calumet cult. The rest of the world, meanwhile, enjoys tobacco any way it can, largely undisturbed by such scruples.

2

Tobacco: To Virginia and across the Appalachians, 1492—1792

From its first contact with the Spanish that October day 1492 in the Bahamas, tobacco, until then quite unknown in the Old World, encircled the globe in little more than a century, largely through the agency of traders and sailors who carried the weed and the habit of using it in various ways throughout the world. The three centuries of colonial wars among the European powers following the discovery of tobacco greatly accelerated its diffusion. The plant reached Spain and Portugal by 1558, France the next year, Italy by 1561, and England in 1565. There smoking tobacco in fragile clay pipes took the fashionable young men of that country by storm, to such an extent that a few years after its introduction it was estimated that there were in London alone as many as 7,000 tobacconists doing an annual retail trade of more than 300,000 pounds. At one point the cost of a pound of tobacco to the consumer reached the 1974 equivalent of $500.[1]

Thus by the time English settlers reached Virginia in 1607 and established Jamestown on a permanent basis, they had left behind them in England a ravenous appetite for *N. tabacum* that was limited only by the Spaniards' virtual monopoly of this much-prized strain of Caribbean leaf and by the mercantilist hatred of importing costly stuffs from rival economic powers. In Virginia, where the native Powhatans were smoking a Kinnikinnick they called "uppowoc" (the unacceptable *N. rusticum*), John Rolfe (and *not* Sir Walter Raleigh, to whom most of the credit is given) saw an opportunity and a challenge for the struggling colony. If seed of *N. tabacum* could be transported out of Spanish-held Cuba (illegally, of course) and cultivated successfully, the colonists would have a cash crop for exportation to England that could make the mother country independent of the Spanish tobacco monopoly and at the same time provide a solid economic base for the new settlement. Rolfe managed to get the seeds, they were sown, and tobacco flourished in the Virginia Plantation from the earliest times, soon becoming the foundation of Jamestown's economy. The colony exported some 20,000 pounds of leaf to England by 1618; by 1664 the total had grown to 24 million pounds, and Maryland, Pennsylvania, and the Carolinas were raising tobacco for trade with the home country.

The growing home market for tobacco was from the first, however, threatened by opponents of its indiscriminate use for pleasure. Puritans attacked the enjoyment of tobacco products as a sensual indulgence and as an addictive narcotic comparable to alcohol (which, after all, it is). Social critics remarked that smoking and snuffing are dirty habits the practice of which is offensive to others who are not so addicted. Medical men, who rec-

1. Tobacco reached Turkey in 1605, Russia in 1634, and Arabia in 1663. Spaniards carried the seed to the Philippines, where tobacco was grown and shipped to China, whence it penetrated Siberia and crossed the Bering Sea to Alaska and the Eskimo. That completed tobacco's world-encircling journey. Meanwhile, leaf reached the blacks of Australia, the Hottentots, even the Andaman Islanders; and along the west coast of Africa it came to be much in demand by natives engaged in the slave trade.

ognized the affinity between nicotine and the toxic alkaloids present in such powerful drugs as henbane and nightshade (to which botanical family tobacco belongs), wished the use of tobacco confined to medicinal purposes.

At the same time, leaf was early recognized as a lucrative trade and as a prime source of governmental revenue through taxes, customs and excise duties, and other means. King James I, for example, although one of tobacco's most redoubtable opponents and the author of a particularly virulent diatribe against smoking, *Counterblaste to Tobacco* (London, 1604),[2] was by no means averse to profiting from its sale in England, and besides taxing leaf at a good round rate, sold the retail monopoly for £15,000 a year and promptly raised the price to £20,000. For a long time before the American Revolution British customs collected an excise tax of two shillings a hogshead on all leaf shipped from the colonies. Exports from Virginia alone in the years 1752–1789 ranged between 58,000 and 70,000 hogsheads, each weighing by then about 1,000 pounds,[3] on which the Exchequer annually realized between £200,000 and £300,000 in various duties. International trade regularly provided the mother country with an additional £1,500,000 from American tobacco, since only about half of the leaf imported from the colonies was consumed at home, and the remainder was sold abroad. In 1775 a shipment of 131 hogsheads of leaf worth a little over £1,300 to a Charlestown, South Carolina, proprietor, cost about £4,900 by the time it was sold in England at a

2. James I was, I believe, the first to record that cadavers of smokers, when dissected, revealed lungs coated with tobacco soot.

3. In an effort to evade the full effect of the hogshead tax, Virginia planters had gradually increased their size and weight from about 600 pounds to 1,000, and in some cases to 1,300 pounds. Planters and distillers have always been chary of paying duty.

modest profit to the importer. All the rest of the delivered cost consisted of charges for freight, cooperage, cellarage, insurance, loading, and landing, as well as for excise duties, which came to nearly £ 3,200. No wonder there was a revolution!

Meanwhile, the cultivation of *N. tabacum* was proceeding apace in the Mid-Atlantic states during the century-and-a-half between the founding of Jamestown and the settlement of Kentucky; agricultural practices were being refined to suit different soils and growing conditions; methods of harvesting, curing, and processing leaf for sale were evolving; and a variety of tobacco strains were slowly being differentiated by a curbstone sort of artificial selection. Well before the Revolution, for example, fine Maryland Orinoko was fetching fancy prices in England, and a variety called "Burley," after the plantations of Lord Burleigh where legend has it that this leaf was first grown, was already being generally planted in the Tidewater. It was to prove remarkably fertile and adaptable genetically, and from it have been evolved a host of leaf strains.

Generally speaking, virgin woodland was selected for tobacco-raising once a fallow crop had been sown to stabilize the soil chemistry; and year after year this practice continued, thus decimating the eastern woodlands and depleting the soil, for tobacco is a demanding plant. Even as late as 1800 only the most informed and far-sighted farmers were rotating their crops with legumes and, in those days before commercial fertilizers, few were using manures intelligently or plowing under cover crops to replenish soils. Fresh timberland was chosen not only because it was rich but also because it provided lumber for houses, barns, and rail fences, and the tops and brush could be piled upon the site picked for the seedbed, or "patch," and then burned to kill weeds and insect larvae and to provide needed potash. In March or April, depending on the region, and after the seedbed had been prepared by

27

repeated plowing, hoeing, and raking in order to reduce the soil to a fine texture, the almost invisible tobacco seeds were scattered broadside over the patch, often in the old days mixed with lettuce and mustard seed to protect the young seedlings against the fly and other insects. Then the seedbed was covered (now with muslin or plastic, then with brush) until the danger of frost had passed and the seedlings, now uncovered, had from three to five leaves about the size of a dollar bill.

By this time, the fields had been laboriously readied to receive the new seedlings, each one of which had to be pulled from the seedbed and replanted in hills or in rows. The labor required to prepare these fields, even after the timber and undergrowth had been cut and removed, must have been Herculean. Stumps and rocks had to be removed, the earth plowed, turfs and clods broken up, and the soil worked deep and fine with hoe and mattock before being drawn up into hills or rows ready for the seedlings from the patch.

Then late in April or in May transplanting began, in showery weather in the old days, with watering cans later, and now often with tractor-drawn machines on which men sit to plant the seedlings in prepared holes, after which the hole is closed and water and fertilizer added, all automatically. When Kentucky was settled, however, and until very recently, the seedlings were pulled from the patch by hand, placed in a basket, and immediately planted in the field with the aid of a short stick, pointed at one end, which was inserted into the hilled-up earth to make a hole into which a seedling was placed, and the plant firmed by hand or foot. Another worker followed along to water, or else spring rains supplied the want. Like so many other operations in tobacco cultivation, planting has always been a process that mobilized the farmer's entire human resources. Men and women, grown-ups and children, blacks and whites, farmers, slaves, indentured servants, and tenants all turned out to set the plants in the spring, to hoe and weed throughout the summer and to pick off and kill insects and the great green tobacco caterpillars that attack the vulnerable leaves, to "top" or cut off the flower heads in midsummer, and then to pull off "suckers" (little second-growth leaves that appear at the juncture of the great leaves and the stalk) which rob the leaves of nourishment after the plant has been topped.

As the plants mature and the leaves take on an increasingly yellow hue, certain varieties and certain methods of cultivation required that the ripe leaves be "primed," or removed one by one and by hand, allowed to wilt in the sun, and then taken in, stitched together or otherwise attached to four-foot long stakes called tobacco sticks and then placed between the beams and rafters in a special barn for curing. Over the years, curing came to be done in a variety of different ways appropriate to the steadily diverging evolution of different leaf strains. Thus the Bright-leaf of Virginia and North Carolina is cured by heated flues in the barns (hence the name Flue-cured tobacco), while the dark, Fire-cured leaf of Western Kentucky is dried (and flavored) by smoke and heat from open hickory fires in tightly chinked barns. White Burley and Air-cured dark leaf, on the other hand, are cured in barns with louvers that open to the hot, dry air of the Kentucky autumn. But then, White Burley is ordinarily not primed in harvest. Rather, the whole plant is allowed to ripen in September's heat, often attaining a height of six feet or more, when crews of workmen move into the dense rows of yellowing plants and cut them down through the main stalk near the ground, split it and impale the entire plant on a tobacco stake along with several others. After a brief initial wilting in the field, the plant-laden stakes are carried in to the curing barn and hung, the tall, narrow shutters along the sides opened to welcome the dry October air that gently cures the leaves to the dryness of onionskin—and to onionskin's fragility and inflammability.

The cultivation and air-curing of White Burley was for Kentucky's first settlers of 1774 still a century away; but the broad outlines of the cultural technology of Burley leaf had already become established in Virginia and was carried whole into Kentucky. Thus the cool, overcast, rainy months of the winter could be counted on to bring the dry and brittle leaves into "case," a still-used term that means a proper degree of moisture content that enabled the cured leaf to be handled without breaking. It was then, usually on a rainy day, that the stakes were taken down from the rafters and drawn out of the plants, the leaves stripped from the stalks, tied in "hands," and stored on a flat wooden frame to "sweat" for a while. Then the sweated leaf was prized under great mechanical pressure into a huge oaken barrel called a hogshead which when full could hold a half-ton or more, a lid was fitted on and secured, and the whole reinforced with hoops. The hogshead was then ready for shipment to market.

In colonial and backwoods America, shipment to market was by no means a simple process, for roads were largely trails, railways had not yet been invented, rivers were undredged, and canals still to be dug. Manhandling a half-ton hogshead of valuable leaf even the shortest distances became a formidable task. Fortunately, the geography of Tidewater Virginia made the movement of massive objects like hogsheads relatively easy, since much of the region is open to the sea or to tidal estuaries or is deeply penetrated by rivers navigable by the shallow-draft sailing vessels of the seventeenth and eighteenth centuries that would carry the leaf to foreign markets. Beyond and on either side of the rivers were streams capable of handling rafts, barges, and other flat-bottomed craft that could bring hogsheads downstream to the warehouses established at the head of navigable waters. Under the auspices of the colonial government, public warehouses were established to receive, inspect, store, and ship leaf to factors in England.

More important for such a delicate and valuable commodity as tobacco, the quality control of which is crucial, a cadre of licensed public leaf inspectors was established early on. They broke open the hogsheads, examined the leaf, and either certified the quality of the contents or, if they found it deficient, ordered it burned. After a further inspection and replacement of the leaf in the hogshead, a final weighing, and storage awaiting the next ship from England, the warehouseman issued a note to the grower for the quantity of his tobacco; and money would be duly credited to an account in England when, months later, the shipment of hogsheads was received, duties paid, and the leaf sold.

Given the slow communications of that day, this was a time-consuming process; and the time between leaf harvest and payment to the planter could be years. In addition, money was scarce in the colonies and almost non-existent on the frontier. In consequence, tobacco generally, and more particularly the warehouse notes issued upon receipt of hogsheads accepted for shipment to England, passed for money in the colonies and later in the frontier states. Fines at law were payable in leaf or warehouse notes.[4] Anglican vicars were commonly paid in leaf, and debts, taxes, and commercial transactions were settled by barter in tobacco or by assignment of warehouse notes at a value fixed by law. Indeed, tobacco became all but legal tender, and legislatures regulated the rates in tobacco leaves that could be charged by taverns and public houses, tailors, parish and county rates, and the like.

The original white settlers of Kentucky came through gaps in the Appalachian Mountains from Virginia and North Carolina, and more latterly down the Ohio River

4. Illegally introducing a Quaker into Virginia, for example, was at one time punishable by a fine of 5,000 pounds of leaf, which should give a fair idea of the anathema in which a wetback Friend was held by pious Anglican settlers!

from Pennsylvania, bringing with them the institutions, customs, and agricultural practices of their homes on the Eastern Shore—but with a settled antipathy to the plantation system they had left on the other side of the Smokies. In their largely agrarian economy, the cultivation of tobacco held a central place: indeed, the search for fresh land to replace the exhausted Tidewater soil was a principal motive in the minds of the pioneers. Beginning as a trickle that grew into a stream and then a flood, they washed into the Central Bluegrass as far as the Kentucky River, lapped south to Tennessee and north to Maysville and the Ohio River, west as far as the Falls at Louisville, and then down the Ohio and more southerly into the Barrens and Pennyrile, where they encountered the rich bottomlands along the Tennessee and Cumberland rivers flowing toward their confluence with the Ohio near what is now Paducah.

In wagons, on horseback, or afoot, they brought with them the tools and seeds with which to reconstitute the society they had left behind: hoes, plows, axes, guns, spinning wheels, churns; flax for linen and linsey-woolsey, wheat and rye for flour, corn for meal and feed, hemp for fiber and to "fallow" virgin woodlands for other crops, and an ounce or two of "Burleigh" seed.

For the first few years after a permanent settlement was established near what is now Harrodsburg, life was lived on a subsistence level as woods were felled, log houses and barns were built, fields cleared and enclosed with split-rail fences, protective stockades erected, and rude towns and roads laid out, the latter usually following aboriginal buffalo trails. Even so, by the mid-1780s the deep, fertile soil of Kentucky allowed the settlers to enjoy a production of crops and livestock in excess of what could be consumed at home, even with the growing influx of new settlers and a rapidly rising population.

Casting about for a market for their surplus of commodities, Kentuckians found themselves in a dismaying dilemma, for there were no markets to be reached with the bulky stuffs the land produced. Across the Ohio, the land was occupied by Indians, trappers, and renegades, as it was beyond the Mississippi and Missouri. The Eastern marketing centers lay across the roadless fastness of the Appalachians or were reachable up the Ohio at Pittsburgh; in either case a difficult and dangerous journey of not less than three months was required. Nothing was possible in that direction until steamboats could make the Ohio easily navigable upstream and railroads could penetrate the mountains many years later.

One other direction for trade remained, that to the south and to the Spanish-occupied port of New Orleans, by way of the Ohio and Mississippi rivers, where there was a direct outlet to the ports of Europe and the East Coast. This opportunity was not lost on Kentuckians raised in the Tidewater, who were accustomed to thinking in terms of heavy transportation of agricultural goods by water rather than overland. They saw that Kentucky's midcontinental geography nearly duplicated that of Virginia, though on a vastly grander scale: from the Big Sandy on the east to the Mississippi, navigable rivers cut deep into the region's plains and highlands— the Kentucky, the Green, the Cumberland, and the Tennessee, the last two of which drained the great central basin of Tennessee. Already (once again following the commercial and agricultural practices developed in Tidewater Virginia over nearly two centuries) warehouses were going up along the lower reaches of the Kentucky River, goods collected, barges loaded in the wet season of the spring when snags and sandbars and the Great Falls of the Ohio at Louisville could be traversed in safety, and the long journey downriver begun in hopes of trade, profit, and an established market. But trade south by river was at best a chancy affair, beset by marauding Indians, renegade white pirates, and constantly changing channels and water levels along the streams. Moreover, if the barges arrived safely at Natchez or New Orleans, their cargoes often were seized by the Spanish customs authorities, who had erected an export barrier to American products bound for Europe as a means of protecting the trade of their own colonies in the New World.

What was needed, then, was a way of opening the door to Europe for Kentucky products offered by New Orleans. An opportunity presented itself, and an opportunist capable of taking advantage of it, in the spring of 1787, midway through the interminable and Byzantine complexities of Kentucky's negotiations to achieve independence from Virginia. The opportunist appeared in 1784 in the person of James Wilkinson, who at twenty-seven years of age was a hugely ambitious and not overly scrupulous man of positively baroque personality and talent for conspiracy. Of obscure origins, Wilkinson had made a brilliant marriage to Anne Biddle, of the Philadelphia Biddles, and had rapidly run through the handsome dowry his bride had brought with her. He had earlier turned his hand to military adventure by embarking with General Benedict Arnold upon the abortive Quebec campaign of 1775. Emerging from service in the Continental Army as a brigadier general, Wilkinson set out to recoup his fortune on the frontier of Kentucky; and two years after setting up shop in Lexington he headed west and settled on one of the few extensive flood plains which interrupt the escarpment flanking the Kentucky River, at a point near the head of navigation on that torturously winding stream. There in 1786 he built and opened a warehouse—incidentally founding what is now Frankfort, the pleasant site of the capital of the Commonwealth—hired one Peyton Short as his agent, and issued fulsome brochures inviting farmers, merchants, and manufacturers of Central Kentucky to bring their goods to him and promising handsome profits in trade with Louisiana and the Spanish.

By no means a stupid man, Wilkinson was able to pay

off on his promises. While the Kentucky River was an unreliable avenue of commerce until it was cleared and channeled many decades later, during the spring floods it was possible for shallow-draft flatboats to clear the snags and bars, reach the Ohio River, and run the rapids at the Falls of Louisville. To defend against attack by Indian raiding parties and white river pirates along the Ohio and Mississippi, Wilkinson heavily armed his flatboats and formed them into flotillas or convoys, which enjoyed the safety of numbers from even the most determined assault. In addition, these vessels were crewed by an awesome lot of riverboatmen like the legendary Mike Fink, a brawling, drinking, womanizing, braggadocio breed of bruisers whose feats of strength and love of fighting and carousing have since become a part of the folklore of mid-America.

So manned, disposed, and equipped, Wilkinson and his little fleet set out from Frankfort in April 1787, loaded with Kentucky hams, bacons, flour, salt, hogsheads of tobacco, and other farm products bound for New Orleans. After a journey downstream of about a month marked by every conceivable danger and misadventure, the convoy reached Natchez and was promptly seized, lock, stock, and hogshead, by the Spanish authorities there and confiscated in the name of the Spanish crown. Highly secret "conversations" then ensued between the devious Wilkinson and the Spanish governor of the Louisiana Territory in New Orleans, Esteban Miro, with the result that by the end of June or the beginning of July the fleet and its cargo were released and made New Orleans. There, after paying the Spanish entry duty, the goods were unloaded and sold advantageously.

Whether by threats of war if such a sizable American cargo were confiscated by the Spanish, or by the tantalizing prospect of delivering the restless settlers of Kentucky to the Spanish colony—they were already agitating for secession from Virginia and were by no means determined to join the unstable union of the thirteen Atlantic Coast states—Wilkinson so far carried the day with Governor Miro that he not only got his boats and cargo released and sold,[5] but came away with an agreement that he would have a monopoly on all trade between Kentucky and Louisiana. In return, he was placed on the diplomatic payroll of Spain as Secret Agent 13 and sworn to allegiance to the Spanish crown. He then returned to Kentucky, finally reaching Frankfort in February 1788, where he was received as very much the conquering hero who had opened the ports of the East Coast and of Europe to the produce of Kentucky. Appropriately enough, he arrived resplendent in a coach and four!

Once back, Wilkinson threw himself into the task (which was to prove unsuccessful) of solidifying his position as monopolist of Kentucky's trade with Louisiana and expanding his warehouse business, meanwhile participating in the political intrigues that were swirling around the growing agitation for Kentucky's independent statehood (whether within or outside the union) and freedom from the yoke of Virginia's dilatory and absentee government. Throughout the eight years and ten conventions that it took before statehood and admission to the newly formed federal union were finally achieved on June 1, 1792, Wilkinson and his agent Peyton Short appear to have been deeply (if clandestinely) involved in what came to be called "The Spanish Intrigue,"

5. As was customary then, the 50–60 ton vessels were broken up and sold for timber at the end of the downriver journey, for they were too awkward to make the return trip upstream. Their crews took the overland route to Kentucky along the Natchez and Nashville traces to Louisville. A house in Maysville, largely built of the beams and boards of a flatboat from Pittsburgh, is still standing. Such profligacy with timber by our ancestors helps us to understand how, with the considerable help of tobacco planters, Kentucky's vast forests have so largely disappeared.

which was designed to deliver Kentucky and the other emerging states west of the Appalachians for annexation to Spain's Louisiana Territory. While Wilkinson was downriver on his first trading expedition working out the deal with Miro, Short was back in Danville at the fifth convention, beginning September 17, 1787, representing Wilkinson's grandiose scheme among the members of the "Court" party, who opposed the Federalist "Country" party's program for immediate separation from Virginia and admission to the Union. The Court party, so named because its leaders, John Brown, Benjamin Sebastian, and Harry Innes, were judges, wished rather that Kentucky gain independence as a state, that the Mississippi be opened for trade with Kentucky, and that the state then bargain with the Union and the Spanish for the best terms of affiliation.

Obviously, in this political context, Wilkinson's opening of New Orleans to trade with Kentucky was a great victory for the Court party, particularly in the light of Kentuckians' suspicion that the earlier Spanish withdrawal of Americans' "right of deposit" in New Orleans and closing that port to trade down the Mississippi River had been the result of a secret deal made by the hated Easterner John Jay in return for trade advantages for the seaboard states. Furthermore, the original Confederation was dissolving to make way for ratification of a new constitution and union, although it was anybody's guess whether or not the states would ratify or go their separate ways; the lame-duck Continental Congress was dilatory about statehood for Kentucky; and the impatient frontiersmen suspected that the states of the eastern seaboard were quite uninterested in being joined by a remote state on the other side of the nearly impassable Appalachians.

"The Spanish Intrigue," then, had a lot going for it; and in the sixth and seventh conventions during 1788, while Virginia considered and then ratified the new constitution and threw in with the Federal Union, Wilkinson's intrigues among the delegates for annexation by Spain—promoted by glittering vistas of expanding trade and wealth for the state—all but reduced the assemblies to chaos. The "grandiose but impossible scheme" for annexation (and, incidentally, for power, prestige, and riches for Wilkinson) seemed about to carry the day, when, on the floor of the eighth convention late in 1788, John Brown, one of the leaders of the Court party, rose to speak, and dramatically betrayed Wilkinson's conspiracy with Spain to the Assembly, denounced Wilkinson, and avowed his own support for union with the United States. Confusion in the assembly ensued and charge and countercharge were exchanged, but the day of the Spanish Intrigue had come and gone; for at about the same time the Virginia Assembly passed enabling legislation with generous terms for Kentucky's statehood and union, and almost a year later passed yet another bill for the same purpose (the fourth so far), thus pointing the Commonwealth on the path to unification. There were still three more conventions to go before Kentucky's formal admission to the union was approved by Congress on February 4, 1791, and signed by President Washington; and the indefatigable Wilkinson was a prominent if conspiratorial presence at them all, busily promoting a new scheme with Spain, bribing delegates, and intriguing right and left, but by now to little purpose. Hardly more than a year after that, Kentucky became the fifteenth state of the new United States of America.

And not a moment too soon for those who sought Kentucky's admission to the union, for trade with New Orleans was booming, thereby seeming to fulfill Wilkinson's glowing prophecies, and tobacco loomed large in that trade, as did Wilkinson himself. The warehouse and inspection system developed in Virginia had already been carried over the mountains by the settlers of Kentucky; for in 1783 the Virginia Assembly enacted legislation allowing for the establishment of such warehouses and the appointment of official leaf inspectors, fixing a charge of ten shillings per hogshead for each inspection, and stipulating that inferior leaf must be burned, while acceptable hogsheads were receipted by the warehouseman. As in Virginia, these receipts could pass as notes, currency, or negotiable paper and be employed in the payment of public debts at the rate of twenty shillings per hundredweight of tobacco. Nor was Wilkinson's warehouse at Frankfort the first such venture, for in 1783, the very year of passage of the Virginia law, one Colonel Campbell had opened a warehouse in Louisville. But Wilkinson's warehouse was for a short time successful. Besides the ten-shilling-per-hogshead fee for inspection, Wilkinson levied a six-shilling-per-hundredweight charge for freight loaded at Frankfort, or four shillings sixpence if loaded at Louisville. Planters were guaranteed fifteen shillings on their leaf that reached New Orleans (shipping was at the owner's risk, such were the hazards of the journey), and Wilkinson received two-thirds of any overage.

It was a good scheme, like the Spanish Intrigue, and might have worked; but the Fates conspired against both, so interlocked was trade and the political conspiracy. The crucial blow to both enterprises was a Royal Order from Seville to Governor Miro, dated December 1788, opening the ports of New Orleans and Natchez to anyone who paid the Spanish entry duty, thus ending Wilkinson's monopoly on that trade and similarly demolishing his economic argument for annexation to Louisiana. Even so, in January 1789 Wilkinson gathered together at Louisville a great flotilla of twenty-five flatboats and keelboats armed with three-pounder cannon mounted on swivels and crewed by over 150 men. Cargo included hogsheads of tobacco, barrels of meat in brine, smoked hams and bacons, barrels of flour, cornmeal, whisky, salt, gunpowder, hemp, and other stuffs— altogether a huge cargo. And by the next year, 1790, the trade had swollen even more; 250,000 pounds of tobacco, most of it from Kentucky, was received at New Orleans, where it was selling in Spanish coin for the equivalent of $9.50 to $10.00 a hundredweight, in contrast to the $2.50 that leaf was selling for back home.

Unfortunately for him, the end of Wilkinson's profitable trade was at hand, for farmers were reluctant to pay his heavy transportation charges and began to organize their own convoys of flatboats. Then too, the Kentucky River, still unimproved and clogged with snags, bars, fallen timber, driftwood, loggers' dams, and periodic low water, could not be used regularly for heavy, year-round traffic; and the leadership in downriver traffic soon passed to the much more strategically located hamlet of Louisville, at the Falls of the Ohio.

Louisville meanwhile was busily solidifying its position as the state's commercial hub during the 1790s, when it was literally the only port on the Ohio River; and goods like tobacco from Northern and Central Kentucky had to make it there the best way they could for shipment to New Orleans and the ports beyond. By the time of statehood, indeed, Louisville already had its own factories producing tobacco products—"seegars," "smoakum" (pipe mixtures), snuff, and "chaw" (chewing tobaccos).

Nevertheless, the burgeoning prosperity of Kentucky and the place of tobacco in its largely agricultural economy were dependent on a congeries of factors over which Kentuckians had little control. Maintaining free trade and navigation on the Mississippi River clear to New Orleans was essential, of course; but beyond that, unimpeded access to the ports of Europe and the East Coast, where most of the western leaf crop was sold, was no less important. Unfortunately, for nearly a generation after statehood, Kentucky's planters and merchants found themselves at the mercy of international upheavals which profoundly affected the state's economy.

3

The Rising Burley Giant of the West, 1792—1860

THE PROSPERITY anticipated by Kentucky's tobacco planters as a result of the quarter-million pounds of leaf that went through New Orleans in 1790 at high prices was threatened at the end of that year by a decision of Spanish authorities to limit purchases of western leaf to 40,000 pounds annually. Continuing a fine old Virginia tradition, however, Kentucky tobacco planters continued to overproduce, a goodly portion of which no doubt was sold in New Orleans unrecorded by the excisemen, for our Scotch-Irish forebears were dedicated and gifted smugglers and bootleggers. Still, trade downriver was unstable. The mad scheme of "Citizen" Genet and George Rogers Clark to launch a backwoods attack on New Orleans and claim it for the United States in 1793–1794 was only just forestalled by President Washington. If successful, the plot would have wreaked havoc on the frontier.

On the other hand, the Pinckney Treaty of San Lorenzo, concluded in October 1795, guaranteed free navigation on the Mississippi River and duty-free deposit at New Orleans of American goods bound for export, including flour, meat, foodstuffs, and tobacco. A period of unexampled prosperity ensued, and the state's population ballooned from 73,000 in 1792 to some 200,000 by 1800. The uncertain market for leaf in Louisiana after 1791, however, encouraged Kentucky planters to diversify their crops. Thus for the years 1791–1795, while Kentuckians continued to ship between 1,500 and 2,000 hogsheads of leaf downriver, by 1798 the value of shipments of wheat flour from the state exceeded that of tobacco; and by 1803 the dominance of flour had become a settled fact of economic life in the Commonwealth, with brine-packed or smoked meats a close second.

An expanding trade with the American territories to the south was rapidly opening up as well, after Eli Whitney's perfection of the cotton gin in 1793 gave an enormous impetus to the cultivation of cotton in that region. The one-crop economy that resulted needed to be served with livestock, foodstuffs, fibers, and other commodities imported from Kentucky and Tennessee, notably hemp, which was successfully grown in Kentucky from the first and manufactured as bagging for cotton bales, sheeting, floor coverings, even paper, and shipped south.

With all the traffic downriver, boat building rapidly became a major industry in the state, particularly since it was the practice then to break up boats when they reached New Orleans and sell the lumber for construction. Kentucky's seemingly inexhaustible hardwood forests encouraged a lively business along the state's many waterways in "Kentucky broadhorns" (flatboats), oared keelboats, and sweep-steered barges. Again, like the fabled riverboatmen, a no-less raffish breed of drovers established itself here, who made their living driving stock to eastern markets. Pigs, which traveled well, were driven over the Appalachians in early summer to the Potomac, for example, usually reaching there by the first frost. Then too, in 1789, at the Craig-Parker distillery in Georgetown, the process was developed of making bourbon whisky with a sour mash of corn aged in charred-oak barrels. It helped remove foreign particles, darkened the color of the liquid, and mellowed the taste of what the Indians had aptly described as "firewater." More to the point for Kentucky's trade, bourbon was the most profitable and easily transported form in which corn could be merchandized. And wool and flax—even cotton—were grown and manufactured in the state for trade.

Tobacco, however, remained peculiarly sensitive to international conditions, since the principal leaf markets remained in Europe, which was for the twenty-odd years between 1792 and 1815 torn apart by the cataclysmic upheavals of revolutionary warfare, reverberations from which reached Kentucky early on and profoundly affected its agriculture and commerce. The Pinckney Treaty of 1795 was undermined in October 1800, when Spain ceded the Louisiana Territory to France under the secret provisions of the Treaty of San Ildefonso. It was the French foreign minister Talleyrand's plan to occupy the territory as a means of frustrating westward expansion of the United States; but an expedition to garrison the region came a cropper when an effort to establish an advanced base on San Domingo was forestalled by the British. Nevertheless, in October 1802 the Spanish Intendant at New Orleans, Morales, violated the Pinckney Treaty by revoking the Americans' right of deposit. Coming in the midst of the harvest season, with tobacco curing in the barns, the dudgeon of Kentuckians reached heights rarely equaled since; and, with the legislature sitting, Governor James Garrard petitioned President Jefferson for relief. This move expedited Ambassador Robert R. Livingston's negotiations with the French so much that, by April 30, 1803, an agreement to purchase the vast Louisiana Territory for $15 million was concluded between France and the United States.

The Louisiana Purchase assured Kentuckians of a market and an outlet to foreign ports for their produce, but their troubles with foreign trade for tobacco and other staples were far from over. One of the state's first legislative acts following admission to the Union had been a bill adopting the "Virginia system" of warehouses, quality-control inspections, and the issuance of receipted notes on stored tobacco (equivalent to a penny a pound) that could pass as currency in payment of fees, fines, forfeitures, and debts both public and private. Even the practice of burning unacceptable tobacco continued until 1809; thereafter, it was returned to the planter for disposal and could not be repacked. In spite of the continuing uncertainty of foreign markets for tobacco, however, between 1792 and 1810 Kentuckians opened forty-two new tobacco warehouses. Yet as early as 1804 an advertisement in a newspaper sought a buyer for 30,000 pounds of Kentucky tobacco that was between three and four years old, which indicates that tobacco production had already outstripped demand.

As the intensity of the wars in Europe increased, America's foreign trade, of which tobacco was a principal item, declined. Just before the Declaration of Independence, for example, the English colonies in America were annually exporting over 100 million pounds of tobacco to the mother country and elsewhere; but this astonishing figure was not reached again until Washington's first term as president, when in 1791 118,000 hogsheads of tobacco, worth $4,349,567, were shipped, thereby making it the nation's principal export crop. Thereafter, in the 1790s exports fell between 10 and 15 percent. By Jefferson's second term, exports stood at 60 million pounds; between 1811 and 1815, at 40 million pounds; and the low point was reached in 1814, when only 4 million pounds reached foreign ports. Moreover, an ever-increasing share of United States' production of tobacco for home consumption and foreign markets was coming from the western states of those days, Kentucky and Tennessee (and later Ohio, Indiana, and Missouri), perhaps as much as 20 percent by 1820.

The British blockade of European ports and interference with, or outright seizure of, maritime traffic on the high seas, the depredations of privateers, raiders, and pirates, the ebb and flow of warfare in Europe, the Caribbean, Atlantic, and Mediterranean, and a host of governmental enactments in England, France, and the United States—such as Jefferson's disastrous Embargo Act of 1807–1808—spelled chaos and ruin to the young country's essential foreign trade and to its tobacco growers on both sides of the Appalachians. Out of the economic suffering thus engendered, a party of "Warhawks" formed itself in Congress with the purpose of affirming by armed hostilities if necessary the principle of freedom of the seas (and equally important, the freedom and security of the Mississippi Basin) which was a requirement for a successful trade in American export crops such as tobacco. It is not surprising therefore that the leaders of the "Warhawks" should have been largely drawn from the tobacco-growing states of the trans-Appalachian region—notably Henry Clay and Richard M. Johnson from Kentucky, Felix Grundy from Tennessee, and John Calhoun from South Carolina—nor that their impatient, cocksure frontier mentality should have pushed the weak new nation into the military debacle known as the War of 1812, that for a time, once the British had succeeded in blockading our coasts, brought foreign trade to a dead halt and disaster to many planters and merchants. What is surprising, however, is that out of the negotiations to end the war which resulted in the Treaty of Ghent (December 1814), a good many American aims were acknowledged, either explicitly or tacitly: the great central basin drained by the Mississippi River was opened to navigation freely, the desirability of security from Indian attack affirmed, and the basic claims to maritime rights maintained. For a country that had not only been defeated but utterly humiliated, the United States came away from the conference table with more than anyone had a right to expect.

Nevertheless, the twenty-five years of nearly world-wide hostilities which ended in 1815 with the Congress of Vienna had dealt a body blow to Kentucky's tobacco economy from which it did not recover until the 1830s, when leaf achieved rough parity as a cash crop with flour, corn, hemp bagging and rope, livestock and meat, gunpowder, salt, and bourbon whisky. With foreign markets undependable, Kentucky farmers and planters had turned away from the cultivation of tobacco, profitable as it could be, toward produce and husbandry that had a certain and extensive home market—particularly in the cotton states of the Deep South. Kentucky's commerce, then, turned southward, where it remained pointed until long after the Civil War. Thus in 1802 the state's trade downriver totaled $626,673, of which the leading items were 85,570 barrels of flour, 72,000 barrels of dried pork, 2,485 barrels of salt pork, and other commodities, including a few thousand hogsheads of tobacco.

Kentucky was rich in salt licks; thus by 1810 there were thirty-two saltworks in the state which produced 342,970 bushels of salt. Kentucky's thousands of caves yielded an abundance of niter, which mixed with charcoal (from the state's hardwood forests) and sulphur, made gunpowder. In 1810 there were sixty-three powder mills in the state, and production of gunpowder reached 115,716 pounds, with an additional 201,937 pounds of saltpeter. By 1819 Kentucky was shipping 200,000 gallons of bourbon to New Orleans every month; indeed, one Louisville distiller was supplying 1,500 gallons a day.

In 1810, again, there were thirteen mills manufacturing hemp bagging and twine, and thirty-eight rope walks making hemp line and rope for rigging. Production reached 5,755 tons that year. Seven years later, 1 million yards of bagging was shipped south for cotton bales, and a substantial trade in hemp yarn and twine to the eastern states was well established. Indeed, between 1840 and 1870, Kentucky produced nearly all the hemp grown in the United States; and so popular had this crop become that it threatened for a time to make a one-crop state of Kentucky, until declining demand for hemp resulted from the development of steamships and the production of cheaper substitutes such as sisal.

By 1825 tobacco production in Kentucky was rapidly recovering, helped along immeasurably by two interrelated developments in transportation: the entrance into river service of the steam-powered packet boat and the construction of a way around the Falls of the Ohio at Louisville. The first steamboat to reach Louisville was Nicholas Roosevelt's *City of New Orleans* in 1811, on a journey from Pittsburgh to the Gulf. Four years later, in 1815, the *Enterprise* steamed upriver from New Orleans in the then-spectacular time of twelve days, or less than half the twenty-eight days it normally took rafts and flatboats to make the same journey downriver. Thereafter, steam packet-boat service between Louisville and New Orleans and Louisville and Pittsburgh became a regular, and then the dominant mode of transport until the coming of the railroad after 1850. The advent of the steam packet lent new urgency to the elimination of the last major obstacle to navigation on the Ohio, the falls at Louisville, which were passable only in floodtimes, and which required that cargo and passengers be unloaded above or below the falls and transported on land to the other side. The existence of the falls, of course, had been the making of Louisville, which by 1820 was a thriving town of 4,000 and was already an important hogshead tobacco market, warehouse, and commercial center.

As early as December 1804 the state legislature had enacted a bill chartering a canal at Louisville to circumvent the falls, but nothing came of the project, although the arrival of the *Spirit of New Orleans* with its attendant hoopla revived interest in 1811. It was not until 1825 that, under private capital, work on what is now the Portland-Shippingport Canal began in earnest and was carried through to completion by the end of 1830. On December 5 of that year, the Portland Canal was officially opened and the steamer *Uncas* passed through headed downriver.

With this barrier removed, Kentucky's trade with the South boomed. In 1839, a total of 1,500 steamboats and 500 keelboats and flatboats passed through the Portland Canal carrying 300,000 tons of produce. As the great grain-producing states of the Northwest Territory opened up to settlement and navigation was improved on the great streams and lesser tributaries, the character of Kentucky agriculture began to change and to resemble more what it now is. Grain was still grown, but much of it went for livestock feed as Kentucky emerged as one of the great meat-producing states and as a center for the breeding of fine blooded animals. In the Bluegrass, hemp continued to be a staple crop, but these 1838 figures of Bourbon County's trade tell a significant story, for in that year 10,000 cattle were sold, 40,000 hogs, 3,000 horses and mules, $50,000 worth of bacon and lard, and $70,000 of bourbon whisky. Notable absences from this inventory of the county's commodities are tobacco and grains, the latter of which is clearly being marketed in the form of livestock and alcohol.

Tobacco is another story. The center of production of this crop shifted westward as the interior streams such as the Tennessee and the Green and Cumberland rivers were opened to navigation, thus leaving the land-locked Central Bluegrass high and dry.[1] The reason, of course, lies in the great difficulty of moving half-ton hogsheads (by the 1830s they might have weighed as much as 1,300 pounds) from farm to warehouse to market in a

1. Thus Lexington, which once rivaled Louisville as the great city of the state, was dealt a body blow as a result of her remoteness from rivers and, later, railroads, while between 1820 and 1860 Louisville ballooned from a population of 4,000 to over 100,000.

day before railroads, dependable highways, or other forms of heavy transport, which virtually dictated that the land on which tobacco was grown and prized into hogsheads at the curing barns had to be adjacent to navigable streams. If one studies a map showing the river systems of Kentucky, the emergence of the western and south-central regions of the state, together with a narrow band of counties lying along the banks of the Ohio River in Northern Kentucky, as the major tobacco growing regions becomes obvious: only there are to be found broad, deep streams capable of providing navigable water for boats to handle thousands of heavy hogsheads. If one next turns to examine a map showing the distribution of the major tobacco-producing counties of Kentucky at mid-century (fig. 1), this economic fact of life is abundantly demonstrated, for there in Western Kentucky is a great complex of counties, each annually producing more than 1 million pounds of tobacco, the greatest of which—now Daviess, Henderson, Webster, McLean, Christian, and Todd counties—were each growing more than 3 million pounds. In Northern Kentucky, a fan of counties along the great northern bend of the Ohio River from Trimble County on the west to Mason County on the east were also growing tobacco in significant amounts.

This great surge of tobacco production toward Western Kentucky was spurred by factors other than geographical. The settlement of Kentucky, like that of the nation, took a westward direction and, stimulated by President Jackson's purchase of the Cherokee Indian lands in the extreme western corner of the state, was still filling with settlers in the 1840s and after, settlers who looked to tobacco as their cash crop. Then too, the worldwide spread of a taste for tobacco was continuing and demand growing, so that, after the end of the Napoleonic wars, exportation of this American crop gradually recovered, until in 1840 some 119,500 hogsheads were shipped abroad, exceeding the record year of 1791 for the first time. As early as 1815, the year of the war's end, however, some 90 million pounds had been exported; by the 1830s the annual figure was hovering around the 100 million pound mark: later, in 1860, the figure of 200 million pounds was reached. Moreover, as immigrants poured into the United States, bringing with them from their European homelands a variety of preferences in the use of tobacco, the native market for leaf increased rapidly, until by 1860 fully one-half of each year's crop was marketed for home use, up from only one-fifth in 1830.

Significantly improved strains of the old "Burleigh" were also being developed and grown in the principal south-central counties throughout the pre-Civil War period, and "Red Burley," "Stand-up," "Rainbow White," "Red Twist Bud," and "Little Burley" fetched significantly higher prices than the older, heavier varieties of leaf. Thus as early as 1817, a superior quality of Burley grown in Adair County fetched $8.00 a hundredweight at New Orleans, when other leaf was bringing between $.75 and $2.50; and the cultivation of this new and improved type spread to Logan, Christian, Barren, and other western counties, where Burley tobacco soon became the main cash crop. This was an important consideration, for poor quality leaf grown outside these south-central counties brought low prices in the years 1819–1836 and could have damaged the growing international reputation of, and market for, Kentucky's tobacco. In England, then as now a principal market for American tobacco, Kentucky's Burley was already sufficiently well known and in demand that a system of grading classes, with price differentials, was established like that which had been in effect for many years for Virginia and Maryland leaf, ranging from the top "fine and leafy" through "middling" to the least desirable "ordinary and old"; there was a separate category for stripped tobacco.

The long and the short of it was that, by the 1830s

new and specialized types of tobacco were being developed, overall leaf quality was improving, prices were rising, access to markets was getting better, and Kentuckians were raising more and more tobacco—so much so indeed that by 1839 the state produced around 53 million pounds of tobacco, second only to Virginia. In 1859 Kentucky's production reached 108 million pounds, just 16 million short of Virginia's total. By 1865 Kentucky had become the nation's premier tobacco growing state in poundage, a leadership the state did not relinquish until 1929 (to North Carolina). Whereas in 1830 about a third of the total United States crop of leaf was raised in the "West," between 1843 and 1860 that figure grew to one-half, most of which was grown in Kentucky and Tennessee, although the latter was a distant second.[2]

At the same time, tobacco was generating an ever-growing industry in the cities, among merchants, warehousemen, and manufacturers, who in various ways handled and processed leaf or fabricated tobacco products for sale and use. Reliable statistics are hard to come by before 1850, when the census was reorganized, but we do know that Lexington as early as 1817 boasted three tobacco factories with a total capitalization of $57,000, and Hopkinsville got one the next year. Frankfort remained the principal tobacco market and warehousing town through the first half of the nineteenth century, when the lead passed to Louisville. Between 1815 and 1820 Louisville shipped about 500 hogsheads annually, while Frankfort shipped only 282, worth $14,100, or 50 cents a hundredweight.

At this time a considerable trade in Kentucky tobaccos had become established in the center of the manufac-

2. In 1839 Kentucky led the nation in hemp production, and ran a close second to Tennessee, which was also supplying the Deep South, in corn and hogs, besides being near the top in tobacco, wheat, and beef.

turing district, which was, and remains, Virginia and North Carolina. While some processing and manufacture of tobacco was carried on in the state, the bulk of the crop was still being shipped to New Orleans, and there either loaded on ships for Europe or, more and more, on coasting vessels bound for Virginia or the New York-New Jersey area, the nation's cigar and snuff manufacturing capitals. In Danville, Lynchburg, Richmond, and Petersburg, Virginia, not only were tobacco products manufactured for home consumption (coming back into Kentucky to be sold as finished goods), but there the vital processes of stripping, stemming, and redrying were carried on prior to manufacture or to being shipped to factories farther north or in Europe.[3] There also were the huge complexes of warehouses for the storage in hogsheads of tobacco which had gone through these preliminary stages and were awaiting manufacture after one or two years of aging.

Thus when the old antebellum trade and census figures mention "tobacco factories" in Kentucky, no one can say with any assurance what proportion were processing plants involved in stripping, stemming, and redrying for storage, and what were manufacturing plants. One thing we do know, however: a thriving tobacco industry in the western states—notably in Kentucky, Tennessee, Ohio, and Missouri—was already in being and growing by leaps and bounds by the later 1830s. By 1850 Louisville alone had eighty-two tobacco and "seegar" factories, the annual value of whose products exceeded $1.4 million. Only foundries and "porkhouses"

3. A delicate plant, tobacco was taken out of its hogshead, stemmed (the stems removed), and then dried, after which a precise level of moisture was added to the leaf before it was repacked in hogsheads for the one or two years of controlled fermentation in storage required to bring it to the mellowness necessary for manufacture. In rough outline, these same steps are still followed.

did a bigger business. Two years later, Louisville conclusively asserted its new-found dominance as the state's hogshead market and warehouse capital by shipping 16,000 hogsheads of leaf, or well over 1.6 million pounds. So lively was the trade that year, in what had already become the city's leaf processing and merchandising district along Main Street west of Eighth, that 244 hogsheads of prime light Mason County leaf sold in a single day (May 8) for between $1.50 and $7.05 a hundredweight, or, at a conservative guess, nearly a half-million dollars.[4]

A glance at the 1850 census figures on manufactures of Kentucky counties contains some eye-popping revelations, for with few exceptions they are closely tied to the cultivation and processing of tobacco. Thus Jefferson County's total value of manufactured goods was, at $11,002,103, about nine times that of the nearest rival, Fayette County's $1,338,216. Indeed, Louisville's tobacco manufactures of $1.4 million alone exceeded the total products of any other Kentucky county. The counties of Central Kentucky were not only rich in agricultural goods but were also carrying on a lively manufacturing trade. Of the thirty-four counties out of the state's then total of 100 which produced manufactured goods worth more than $100,000, twelve of them were in the Bluegrass: Fayette, Woodford, Franklin, Mercer, Fleming, Jessamine, Scott, Lincoln, Bourbon, Boyle, Har-

4. Readers familiar with the relatively brief season of today's Burley auction sales in Kentucky, which runs from the last week of November until the latter half of January, may be surprised that leaf was still being sold as late as May; but in the last century tobacco was brought to market any time from November to June. Since then the sale season has continually been shortened as more efficient methods of transporting, handling, selling, and storing leaf have been evolved. The development of the loose-leaf auction and the rapid sing-song of the auctioneer has speeded things up.

rison, and Madison, in that order. Mason County, at $1,064,746, was third in the state, followed by Kenton ($866,964), Campbell ($403,815), and Boone ($132,000), all tobacco counties. Quite astonishing are these manufacturing figures from tobacco-growing counties along the northern Ohio River: Henry County ($435,292), Trimble ($199,770), Shelby ($381,578), and Carroll ($133,663). Except for Meade, Bullitt, and Nelson counties, all the remaining leaders in manufactures were heavy tobacco-growing counties in newly settled Western Kentucky, where there were already large concentrations of warehouses and factories for processing leaf and for the manufacture of plug, twist, cigars, snuff, and smoking mixtures. Paducah and McCracken County had surged to fifth place in the state's manufactures with a whopping $652,740, Princeton and Caldwell County were not far behind at $510,180, and Christian County (Hopkinsville) chalked up a respectable $318,096. Neighboring Trigg (Cadiz) and Todd (Elkton) counties respectively recorded totals of $199,770 and $175,893, and Breckinridge, Meade, and Daviess counties stood above or just below $150,000.

Ten years later, the census figures for the state showed that, in 1860, Kentucky produced a total of $37,931,240 in manufactures, of which nearly $3 million consisted of tobacco products turned out by some ninety-one establishments employing 1,865 people (out of a total factory work force of 21,258). It is clear that Kentucky was still a largely agricultural state, for the leaders in the state's manufactures continued to be flour and meal, at $6,791,164 more than twice the value of tobacco products, and provisions (including meats), at $4,351,575. Tobacco products, in third place among manufactures, stood just ahead of lumber, at $2,935,677.

In the same year, 1860, Kentucky's production of 108,126,840 pounds of tobacco (more than double that of 1850) constituted about one-quarter of the nation's total crop of 434,209,461 pounds and was worth about one-half the cash income of the state's farm population.[5] The leader in tobacco cultivation remained Christian County, which produced almost 11.5 million pounds of leaf, followed by Henderson, with about 8 million, Daviess with 5.3 million, Todd, 4.9 million, and Graves, 4.38 million. Those counties over 3 million pounds included Trigg, Logan, Hopkins, and Caldwell; over 2 million were Barren, Bracken (in the northeast), Breckinridge, Calloway, Cumberland, Ohio, Owen, Union, Warren, and Webster. In short, all but one of the major tobacco-growing counties in the state were in the western portion. And of the state's total of 108 million pounds, over 98 million pounds was raised in the forty-two westernmost counties.

The enormous increase in the market for tobacco, and the consequent boost in its production, not only in Kentucky but in all leaf-growing states, cannot be fully accounted for by increased usage abroad and by rapidly increasing population at home, many of whom were heavy users of leaf in one form or another. Important as these factors were, the decisive force at work pumping up leaf production and consumption was a national change in taste for the form in which Americans most preferred to enjoy tobacco. In a nutshell, nineteenth-century America was the heyday of the "chaw," the ochre-stained beard, the dark, ground-down teeth, and the arching brown trajectory of expectoration leaping through the air on its way to a (hopefully) safe home in the dank depths of the omnipresent spittoon. Not to put too fine a point on it, in the 1800s most Americans who used tobacco chewed it, not only in the backwoods and

5. Besides Virginia, the leader at 123,968,312 pounds, other important leaf-growing states included Tennessee (43,418,097 lbs.), Maryland (38,410,965 lbs.), North Carolina (32,853,250 lbs.), Ohio (25,092,581 lbs.), and Missouri (25,086,196 lbs.). Connecticut, Massachusetts, and Pennsylvania were each raising over 12 million pounds of cigar leaf, and Indiana and Illinois almost 15 million pounds of Red Burley.

rural areas but in towns and cities as well; and the country was veritably awash in a ruddy sea of tobacco spittle. And chewing takes a very great deal of tobacco indeed, a large part of it the various dark and light Burleys of Kentucky.

To understand fully the impact of this phenomenon on the tobacco industry as a whole, from farm to factory, requires us to turn back in our story to pick up the history of the taste for tobacco and the various ways, over the centuries, which people hit upon to enjoy the mildly narcotic properties of treated leaf. One of the wry ironies of Europeans' romance with the New World has been their utter lack of imagination or inventiveness in dealing with tobacco. It is not merely that we still use leaf in ways originated by American natives, but that traditional national preferences in tobacco products have been largely dictated by the way in which leaf was enjoyed by the aborigines first encountered by each nation's explorers and settlers. Thus the Spanish, who were introduced to the cigar by natives of the Caribbean Islands and Central America, have dutifully continued to prefer Havanas during the centuries since. The French court of the seventeenth century, on the other hand, made snuff so *de rigeur,* following the introduction of tobacco by Thevet and Nicot to France in the time of Catherine de Medici, that the practice was slavishly copied by the *beau monde* of every principality in Europe—the elaborate social ritual of the costly snuff box, the sniffed pinch followed by a sneeze, and then a great to-do about the nose and mouth with a lace-trimmed handkerchief. The English, however, took to pipe-smoking, largely because the Amerindians they first met in North America enjoyed tobacco in that form.

Of course, colonial and dynastic wars among the great European powers during the sixteenth, seventeenth, and eighteenth centuries hopelessly mixed up this initially simple picture of national tobacco preferences, as the English, French, Spanish, Italian, German, Austrian, and Scandinavian soldiers, sailors, traders, and diplomats freely exchanged among themselves a taste for smoakum, snuff, and cigars which their descendants brought with them as settlers of the New World. An important principle in the history of tobacco was thus early established: warfare has been the single most significant influence on the worldwide propagation of a taste for *N. tabacum*. The Low Countries, Scandinavia, and Middle Europe, for example, were much fought over. In consequence they took from the French a fondness for snuff—not sniffed in the manner of the Sun King, Louis XIV, but put into the mouth between gum and cheek and sucked, as it continues to be enjoyed by country women in the South—from the Englishman, his pipe and blended smoakum; [6] and from the Spaniards cigars, a liking for the latter of which unaccountably cropped up in Italy.

By the time of the founding of the American Republic toward the end of the eighteenth century, its citizens were enjoying and beginning to manufacture for home use most of the tobacco products that had found favor in their European homelands. As early as 1760 a young French immigrant, Pierre Lorillard, had set up a snuff mill in New York that became the foundation of a distinguished tobacco company which still bears his name.[7] A little later, German and other Middle European immigrants brought with them the skills to establish in New York and New Jersey what is still a major center of cigar manufacture, although important rivals have arisen in Pennsylvania, California (following the gold rush),

6. The practice of blending a variety of different tobaccos together in pipe mixtures—Maryland for its burning qualities, Virginia Bright-leaf for mildness, White Burley for its ability to hold flavorings, and dark "Turkish" strains for their rich flavor and aroma—was to have an important influence on the development of the modern blended cigarette.

7. Lorillard maintains a cigarette factory in Louisville as well as a redrying and storage facility in Lexington.

and Florida (because of its proximity to Cuba).[8] Pipe mixtures were also widely manufactured. Generally speaking, the inhabitants of the established communities of the eastern seaboard continued the sophisticated tobacco-use practices of the Old World.

To the American backwoodsmen, on the other hand, enjoying tobacco in these ways held little meaning. They were too remote from the manufacturing centers in Virginia and New York for such products to reach them, even if they could have afforded the cost of purchase. Then too, frontier people despised Easterners as effete sophisticates hardly distinguishable from the hated Europeans, degenerate heirs of an exhausted hierarchical tradition. The new spirit of a dawning democracy found embodiment in a new hero, the frontiersman of manly independence and unlettered but exquisite nobility, fiercely if insecurely proud of his equality with any man in any station anywhere, as contemptuous of formal culture as he was ignorant, and crude and vulgar to the last degree. A freeborn American such as he required his own culture and tastes—and his own way of enjoying the leaf he was raising. What more simple than to adapt to his own purposes the ancient Indian practice of twisting leaves of tobacco tightly together into a thick rope about a foot long, which was then back-braided upon itself into a neat package suitable for an overalls pocket? Biting off a piece made a "chaw."

The trouble on the frontier was that, before the erection of curing barns, "twist" chewing tobacco was made up green or was at best sun-dried, thus making it no better than a marginally palatable chaw. Frontiersmen therefore increasingly resorted to the practice of fabricating "sweet plug," so named because leaf was wad-

8. The plight of the sweatshop-bound New York cigar rollers so aroused the reforming muckrakers of the 1890s that they became a leading cause in the enactment of enlightened labor legislation early in this century.

ded into a hole in a stump or log and liberally laced with any handy sweetening agent, preferably alcoholic—brandy, cordial, syrup, sorgo, cane sugar, or the like. After a while the fermented cake was removed and used as a tasty chew—tastier in any event than the raw leaf.

In this way chewing tobacco in the form of "twist" or "plug" was born and soon swept the rural sections of the country, the small towns and hamlets, and made a sufficient lodgement in the cities to require the universal installation of that most obnoxious of instruments, the spittoon. With a few notable exceptions in the Northeast and Southwest, chaw carried all before it. Its advantages to a rural population are obvious. Twist and plug were as cheap and available as home-grown leaf and sweeteners, a nail in a barn or a hole in a log, and the time to perform the simple acts of manufacture. Readily portable, chaw tobacco did not require a piece of fire to light it, in a time before the invention of the safety match. For farmers working far from fire and often near inflammable materials like dry straw or hay, "smokeless tobacco" was necessary. All one had to do was to reach back for a twist or plug (twist was soon sweetened as well), bite off a hunk and slip it into the cheek, and go on working, both hands free for the task before him. Finally, because tobacco is a powerful salivant, chewing kept a hot, sweating, hand-laborer's mouth moist; it provided an instant antiseptic in case of a cut; and, because of its appetite-suppressing properties, it made the long stretch from breakfast at dawn to dinner at noon a little more endurable. No wonder it was so popular in the largely agrarian country of a century ago. The rise to domination of the "chaw" culture over the tobacco industry of the last century may be in part traceable to, and was certainly a powerful influence on, the steadily rising demand for western tobaccos of the Burley type, and particularly Kentucky Burley.

Perhaps in imitation of the success of plug and twist, a

comparable movement in taste was going on in snuffs which increased the use of Burley leaf in them as well. Snuff was gradually ceasing to be snuffed, as it had been in the eighteenth-century courts, and came more and more to be used in the mouth, much like "chaw": that is, a pinch was placed between the lower gum and cheek, and sucked. As with chewing tobaccos, the heavy, dark, sugary Burleys of Western Kentucky found ever-increasing favor among manufacturers of what is now coyly referred to as the "smokeless tobacco." Today some 100 million pounds of snuff is consumed each year in this country, the main ingredient of which remains Kentucky and Tennessee Dark-fired tobaccos; and the trade in these tobaccos continues to be an important industry in the Purchase and Pennyrile.[9]

A number of important consequences for Kentucky's tobacco industry followed this evolution in taste. A greatly increased demand for Kentucky and other western states' production of Burley leaf, which was rapidly becoming mandatory for the manufacture of twist and plug, required that the centers for fabricating tobacco products in New York, New Jersey, and Virginia import larger and larger quantities of this leaf. Until well after the end of the Civil War, western Burley had to be shipped by coastal vessels from New Orleans all the way around the southern tip of Florida and so on up the east coast to Tidewater or mid-Atlantic ports, a costly and time-consuming operation. This in turn made their chewing tobaccos more expensive than brands manufactured closer to the source of supply in the West, and thereby gave an enormous impetus to the creation of new manufacturing centers along the Ohio River Valley

9. The largest native manufacturer of snuff, the United States Tobacco Company, has extensive leaf-handling, processing, and warehouse facilities in Hopkinsville, Kentucky, and Clarksville and Springfield, Tennessee, as well as factories in Nashville and Chicago.

and its tributaries, which, as the century wore on, developed into major rivals of the old established firms on the seaboard.

Meanwhile, a great national cataclysm was fast approaching, and the Civil War was at hand, bringing in its train profound upheaval and change in American life and society, and among these great traumas and revolutions, deeply influential and long-lasting alterations in Kentucky's tobacco industry, with which we must deal in the next chapter.

4

White Burley, the Queen of Plug, 1860–1890

THE OUTBREAK of civil hostilities in 1861 posed difficulties for Kentucky and its tobacco economy at the same time that it offered unimaginable opportunities for expanded trade and manufacture. President Lincoln's strategy of denying to the Confederacy the border states, all of which were heavy producers of tobacco leaf and products, was successful; and Kentucky, which had declared its neutrality early in the secession controversy, was quickly occupied by Union forces who beat off a mismanaged Confederate invasion of the state at Perryville. Kentucky was thus spared the devastation visited upon Virginia and North Carolina. On the other hand, the state's traditional markets were in the cotton-growing region of the Deep South, its trade-route the Mississippi River, and its sea port New Orleans, all of which were in Confederate hands. Trade between North and South was soon cut off by both sides, and a successful Union blockade of New Orleans and the Confederate coast was mounted. Kentucky planters and manufacturers therefore found their produce isolated from their markets at home and abroad. Although traffic in contraband was carried on with the secessionist states throughout the war, smuggling could not sustain the economy achieved by the Midwestern states when firing started in 1861.

Although it is often ignored by Civil War buffs who are blinded by the brilliant ballet of maneuver and tactic performed by Jackson, Lee, Stuart, and the rest in the East, the strategically crucial "Western Campaign" to control the Ohio-Mississippi-Missouri watershed was probably of greater long-term importance to the eventual outcome of the war. Securing the Mississippi River for the Union and capturing New Orleans, the South's most important port, not only cut off the Confederacy from its western allies, rich in men and material, but also opened up trade downriver upon which the economy of the Midwest depended.

The security of the Ohio, Missouri, and Upper Mississippi was quickly obtained by the occupation and garrisoning of Cincinnati, Louisville, and Saint Louis, all important tobacco manufacturing centers. Displaying his perceptiveness and initiative, soon-to-be commanding General U. S. Grant recognized the importance of Paducah, at the confluence with the Ohio of the Tennessee and Cumberland rivers, which drained the entire central basin of Confederate-held Tennessee, and seized the city (another manufacturing and processing hub for western leaf) in 1861. In the spring of 1862 Union forces under Grant's brilliant generalship launched a rapid campaign up the Tennessee and Cumberland rivers—vital to the hogshead tobacco of Western Kentucky—which culminated in the surrender of Fort Donelson and a Confederate army of 15,000, thereby securing the lower reaches of these two streams and incidentally taking two other important tobacco manufacturing towns, Clarksville and Springfield, Tennessee.

With Western Kentucky and Middle Tennessee under federal control, Union attention turned to the Mississippi. New Orleans was blockaded, besieged, and taken; and Grant and Sherman, moving downstream, outfought and outmaneuvered the Confederate army, bottled it up in Vicksburg, and finally captured both town and army early in July 1863, only a day or two before General Robert E. Lee suffered a crushing defeat at Gettysburg. For all practical purposes, the end of the rebellion was in sight. More to our purposes, trade downriver to New Orleans was formally restored on September 23, 1863; and access by water to markets and factories for western tobacco and other commodities was once again available.

Meanwhile, of course, the main hub of factories making finished tobacco products in Virginia was in Confederate hands, along with the most important tobacco acreage in Virginia and North Carolina, much of the latter, indeed, being fought over bitterly and destructively by the armies of the two sides. Thus over half of the nation's noncigar manufacturing capacity, and over 60 percent of its leaf production, were denied to the rest of the country. The slack in production of leaf and finished goods had to be taken up somehow, and the task largely fell to the states bordering the Ohio River—Ohio, Indiana, Kentucky, Missouri, and later in the war, Tennessee, where leaf production skyrocketed and "chaw" factories grew by leaps and bounds. Thus between 1860 and 1870, Kentucky took the leadership over Virginia in leaf production, chiefly because Virginia and North Carolina's 1860 crop of 156 million pounds declined to 48 million while Kentucky's steadily grew. By 1880 the "western tobacco crop" had reached the staggering total of 250 million pounds, up 25 percent over the prewar figure, while the Virginia-North Carolina crop, at 133 million pounds, was still 25 percent below the prewar peak. Furthermore, in the war-created vacuum of manufactured tobacco products from Virginia, western factories entered the marketplace in a big way, and the foundations of the "chaw" giants of the Reconstruction Era were firmly established: Sorg, in Middletown, Ohio; the National Tobacco Works in Louisville; Liggett (later

Liggett and Myers) and Drummond Brothers, in Saint Louis; and important snuff and chaw factories in Clarksville and Springfield, Tennessee.

Through all the war-induced upheavals, Louisville prospered unconscionably, and by the end of 1862 had restored its prewar level of commercial activity. Aided by its strategic location on the Ohio River, it became a major supply center for the Union armies to the south and southwest. By 1865, when on April 29 all restrictions on trade with New Orleans had been removed following Lee's surrender at Appomattox, Louisville's trade reached $51 million, up from $37 million in 1860. Already in 1864 the city had handled 63,000 hogsheads of tobacco, or between 63 and 83 million pounds. By this time, Louisville had become thoroughly established as a major hogshead market and tobacco manufacturing center, and in the years between the end of the war and the turn of the century it averaged 60,000 hogsheads a year.

Furthermore, the fact that Louisville had come through the war not only unscathed, but enormously enriched and commercially more powerful than ever before, while potential rivals further south—Nashville, Chattanooga, Atlanta, Birmingham—had either been devastated or occupied by the Union army, or thwarted by the Confederacy's exigencies, gave the Falls City an advantage in postwar trade with its old markets that it was quick to exploit. The destruction of the slave plantation system of the Deep South's cotton-growing states had brought in its tow the dissolution of the plantation store as the locus of commercial life in rural areas and its replacement by the independent or semi-independent crossroads or hamlet general store. This in turn led to a different mode of trading altogether, in which Louisville took the lead. The era of the "drummer" or traveling salesman for a wholesale house or manufacturer was ushered in; the salesman made the rounds of retail outlets in his territory or on his circuit with his suitcase of samples and catalogs, wrote up orders for goods that were relayed back to the home office for filling and shipping, and made his living off commissions from the sales he made. The great era of the drummer was tied to the rapid development of an interlocking system of railroad networks in the United States during the years immediately preceding, and then following, the Civil War. In this, too, Louisville was well ahead of her rival cities along the Ohio at the beginning of hostilities; but this advantage was to turn out to have, in the postbellum years, a worm in its bud.

Perhaps the single most important reason for Kentucky's relatively good overall showing under the commercial handicaps imposed by the wartime disruptions in its southern trade lay in the fact that the state, and Louisville in particular, were beneficiaries of one of the earliest rail systems among the western states that grew tobacco. The Louisville & Nashville Railroad (L & N) had been chartered by the legislature in 1850 to construct a line linking those two cities along a route which roughly followed the old Louisville-Nashville Trace so much used in earlier days by returning riverboatmen, which was in turn a track that followed a primordial buffalo trail. Construction of the line proceeded slowly, but by 1859 the line between the two cities was completed on a route that took it through Elizabethtown and Bowling Green and thereby put it in touch with the Western Kentucky tobacco belt. At about the same time, an extension to Frankfort linked Louisville and Lexington, whence ran a line of sorts to Cincinnati, where connections to the Middle Atlantic states and the eastern seaboard could be made. A further extension from Bowling Green to Memphis by way of Russellville, Guthrie, and Clarksville, the heart of the "Black Patch" tobacco district, was completed before the commencement of hostilities, and not long thereafter a link-up between Elizabethtown and Paducah was established with crossing side branches running north and south between

Henderson and Guthrie and Owensboro and Russell-ville. Thus the entire tobacco belt and its production of leaf and finished tobacco goods were linked, in however complicated and cumbersome a fashion of rival railroads, prejudicial rates, indirect networks of lines, and even incompatible track widths, with eastern sea-board factories and markets. Kentucky products and commodities could—and in greatly increasing tonnages did—go directly east.

Unfortunately, this shift of the flow of Kentucky's traf-fic from south and west along river systems to north and east along railroad systems exposed the now-rich and in-fluential commercial city of Louisville, sitting astride the avenues of trade carrying Western Kentucky tobacco to the East, with a new and powerful rival for the leaf trade in Cincinnati. For Cincinnati's connections by rail to the East were infinitely superior to those of Louis-ville (whose railroads south and southwest had been repeatedly and heavily damaged by military action dur-ing the Civil War) and were in any event much closer. Whatever Louisville shipped east had to go through Cincinnati, so that the glorious days of receiving prime Mason County Burley for sale and shipment to New Orleans were all over for the Falls City. Thus Louisville watched Cincinnati blossom into a major hogshead mar-ket, together with the Northern Kentucky cities that shared its marketing area. Where before the war Cincin-nati might have handled some 6,000 hogsheads of to-bacco a year, by 1864–1865 it was selling 50,000 and continued to do so. Furthermore, Saint Louis was so much closer to the Western Kentucky tobacco fields than Louisville that its tobacco factories could haul hogsheads of tobacco bought on local markets, or from the barn door (as was the frequent practice downstate), and thereby entirely circumvent Louisville's hogshead market and the lucrative rehandling trade that went with it.

What Louisville sought was a trade war with the envied rival, Cincinnati, and its potential ally and benefactor, Lexington. The weapon chosen was the railroad: whether or not Cincinnati could be prevented by Louisville and the L & N from extending a railroad south through Lexington, Berea, and Knoxville to Chattanooga, thereby opening the rich trade of Central Kentucky and the Bluegrass to the Queen City, along with the even more lucrative opportunities of wholesale connections with Georgia, North and South Carolina, and Alabama offered by a railhead at Chattanooga. The arena was the Kentucky state legislature, which alone had the power of chartering railroads, and the tactics included suborning legislators with bribes and every other dirty trick known to politicians and financiers in the Gilded Age. But for Louisville the result was a foregone conclusion. By 1880 Cincinnati and Lexington had a direct rail link, and the Falls City's commercial fate was written on the cards, the splendid Exposition of 1884 and its "City of Lights" notwithstanding.

The reason for Louisville's commercial defeat by Cincinnati as a major distribution and manufacturing center for the Southeast, and more particularly as the hub of Kentucky's tobacco market (although it has never lost its leadership in tobacco manufactures), lies in a number of factors, not least of which was the wholly unanticipated appearance on the scene in 1864 of a revolutionarily advanced strain of Burley tobacco, which came to be called White Burley, and which radically altered the tobacco industry nationally and effected a profound change in the agricultural economy of Kentucky.

Kentucky White Burley, to the chagrin of patriotic Kentuckians, was not discovered in the Bluegrass State at all, but in Brown County, Ohio, on the farm of a Captain Fred Kautz, near Higginsport, in the spring of 1864. Two of Farmer Kautz's tenants, George Webb and Joseph Fore, were seeding tobacco beds when they ran out of seed, and Fore crossed the Ohio River to the farm of George Barkley in Bracken County, Kentucky, because he heard Barkley had some extra seed of Little Burley that he was willing to sell. Back in Ohio with Barkley's seeds, Fore and Webb planted them in the seedbed to sprout for later transplantation. But when the seedlings were ready for setting in the field, they were destroyed; for while they were sturdy enough, and the leaf was fine textured, they were a dirty yellow in color and so thought somehow to be wrong. Next year, however, George Webb, who had saved some of the seed, set them out on his own farm and watched the plants through to maturity, harvest, and curing.[1] They turned out to be classic White Burley, the plants healthy and thrifty with a creamy stalk and pale green leaves marked by a white vein, of superlatively fine, light texture that cured out to a handsome, almost golden, light tan or cream leaf, which smoked "bitter." [2] Knowing a good thing when he saw it, Webb saved enough seed from this 1865 crop to grow some 20,000 pounds the following year, taking two prime hogsheads to the Cincinnati market, where the new, light, delicate yellow-brown leaf attracted a great deal of attention and drew a handsome price from the buyers. In the next year, 1867, Webb's White Burley won both the first and second prizes for fine cutting leaf at the Saint Louis Fair and Exposition and sold for the astronomical price of $58.00 a hundredweight.

With that the future of this new strain of tobacco was assured, and its cultivation spread rapidly throughout Southern Ohio and Indiana, and more importantly into Northern Kentucky and the Bluegrass, where it proved to be particularly successful. The rapid spread of White

1. Another Brown County, Ohio, farmer, Samuel Ellis, may also have grown this same mutant strain of "bright" Burley in 1865, some think.

2. That is to say, "dry," or lacking the heavy load of natural sugars to be found in Red Burley and the other dark, western strains—a crucial consideration in the later success of White Burley.

Burley into Central Kentucky came not a moment too soon for that region, since the market for its principal crop, hemp, was rapidly dying in the years 1865–1870, and the new leaf proved remarkably adaptable to the higher concentration of nitrogen and calcium in the limestone soil there. Indeed, White Burley positively thrived in the Bluegrass, even on old land that had previously been sown to hemp.

The new leaf had other advantages as well. It could be harvested much more rapidly than other types of tobacco, which had to be "primed," that is, each leaf plucked as the plant ripened from the bottom, for Burley could be "stalk-cut" and the whole plant hung in the barn to cure. Curing White Burley did not require smoking the tobacco over a smoldering hickory fire in a tightly chinked barn, as did the dark-fired tobaccos of Western Kentucky, nor heating the leaf through flues, as did the "Flue-cured" Bright-leaf of Virginia and North Carolina. Rather, White Burley is air-cured in barns with long, narrow, perpendicular louvers or panels that may be opened or closed according to the dryness or moisture of the air. Furthermore, White Burley cured more rapidly in the barns and hence could be brought to market earlier—even before Christmas—and that was a decided advantage to cash-starved, debt-ridden Kentucky farmers of the last century.[3] Indeed, so advantageous has White Burley proved to be, that it is now grown in 119 of Kentucky's 120 counties, and its culture has spread to Tennessee, Alabama, Georgia, North Carolina, Virginia and West Virginia, as well as Ohio and Indiana (see fig. 2).

To account for this spectacular boom in demand for a

3. Even with today's much-truncated sales season, Burley markets close a week or two before Dark-fired leaf sales begin, although western leaf is harvested earlier than Burley. This longer curing period seems to be a function of the larger quantity of natural sugars and oils in dark leaf.

previously unknown strain of leaf, it is necessary to go back in our story to pick up the fortunes of tobacco, and particularly chewing tobacco, during the Civil War. Confederate soldiers were often short of even the most rudimentary supplies; but one commodity they had in abundance was tobacco, for with the blockade the southern states had only a home market for their production of leaf. Being mostly farm boys, many of them tobacco farm boys, southern soldiers could be counted on to have a good supply of twist or homemade plug to trade for needed supplies or luxuries with Yankee soldiers, with whom they fraternized extensively during the frequent lulls between fighting, often exchanging Confederate plug for Union coffee. Thus a taste for sweet twist or plug spread among Union soldiers, who returned home after the war carrying their new-found habit with them, but with a decided preference for a milder, sweeter chew than that they had encountered in between-the-lines bartering. In this way plug chewing tobacco made its postbellum emergence into domination of the "chaw" trade, which was itself already the dominant form of leaf consumption.

The difficulty was that, before the discovery of White Burley, no variety of leaf was capable of absorbing the quite extraordinary quantities of sweetening and flavoring agents—between 17 and 25 percent of the plug's weight as opposed to the 4 percent of the traditional North Carolina flat plug—that was demanded by this new and growing taste. Both the major existing strains, "Virginia Bright" and the dark, gummy Red Burley of the West, were too high in natural sugar content to absorb the heavy doses of adulterants—licorice and sugar (molasses, sorgo, maple syrup)—needed to bring the leaf up to the popular level of sweetness. But White Burley was the answer to a sweet plug manufacturer's dreams, for this light, mild, handsome leaf contained very little natural sugar and could therefore be laced with adulterants and mixed with "Bright" or "Dark" leaf in a plug that suited the public fancy for a cloying chaw. And so, because of its moisture, sweetening, and flavoring retention properties, White Burley became an indispensable ingredient of chewing tobaccos. Indeed, these same properties, once the quality and taste of White Burley had been improved, made it a desirable addition to blends of pipe tobacco, which began to carry sweetening agents in the postbellum years; and for the very same reason, it has become an essential component of the modern blended cigarette—Burley carries the "guck."

Once again, the credit for discovering the potential of Burley for carrying adulterants and additives cannot be given to a Kentuckian, but must go to a young Virginia physician, R. A. Patterson, who was manufacturing plug in Richmond as early as the 1850s and whose "Lucky Strike" brand of Burley plug—so named to capitalize on the popularity of the California gold rush of a few years earlier—became a household word in the years following the end of hostilities. Regular "Richmond Plug" was merchandized with at least 17 percent of its weight in additives, a condition made possible by the heavy use of Burley filler—as much as 40 percent in many cases. Furthermore, fine golden-yellow White Burley leaf was much sought after as the wrapper for cakes of plug for the sake of its attractive appearance.

The discovery of White Burley and its properties, together with the center of its cultivation in the Midwest, Kentucky, and Tennessee, gave further impetus to Western tobacco manufacturers, who were naturally concentrating on the production of plug. By 1870 Kentucky factories turned out over $2 million in manufactured tobacco products, over three-quarters of which was in the form of chaw, smoakum, and snuff; and most of that was made in Louisville. But out of a total national production of almost $72 million, Kentucky's portion was not large. The leaders remained New York, with almost $19 million (over $8 million in cigars and cigarettes and a like amount in chewing, smoking, and snuff); Missouri, with $10 million (almost all in chaw and smoakum); and Virginia, with just over $7 million (90 percent in chewing, smoking, and snuff).[4] In the same year, Kentucky's farms produced over 105 million pounds of tobacco out of a total crop of about 264 million, or about 40 percent. In the Midwest, the factory centers were Saint Louis, which sat on top of the West Kentucky Black Patch, Chicago (directly linked to the Patch by the Illinois Central Railroad), and Cincinnati-Middletown, which drew on the Ohio-Northern Kentucky Burley belt.

Ten years later, the nation's tobacco production was nearly 473 million pounds, of which 171 million, or better than a third, came from Kentucky (see fig. 2); but the state was fifth in the manufacture of plug nationally, trailing Virginia, New Jersey, Missouri, and North Carolina in that order, and ninth in the manufacture of all tobacco products, after Virginia, the leader in poundage (56 million), and New York, the leader in value (over $33 million)—the latter because of her heavy concentration on cigars and cigarettes. Out of a national total of 191 million pounds manufactured, Kentucky produced almost 11 million (about 5 percent), worth $4.7 million, $3.7 million of which was in plug. Of the state total, Louisville accounted for nearly half, 5.2 million pounds worth some $3 million. Covington took the lion's share of the remainder, using 2.5 million pounds (about evenly divided between plug and fine-cut chewing tobacco). Altogether, there were 135 tobacco factories in the state (out of a national total of 7,622) employing 2,771 persons at an annual wage of $565,168. In addition, Louisville received 52,536 hogsheads of tobacco

4. Humiliating as it is to admit, Kentucky stood well down the list of tobacco manufacturing states, after Pennsylvania, Ohio, Illinois, and Michigan.

(compared to Cincinnati's 49,402); [5] Paducah and Hopkinsville handled over 10,000 apiece; and Clarksville, Tennessee, over 16,000. Altogether, 162,037 hogsheads of western tobacco were received on western markets, while 112,265 were sent east (84,836 to New York alone and 11,000 to Richmond). The export trade was equally lively: on hand in Liverpool, London, Bremen, and Antwerp were over 87,000 hogsheads of American tobacco, the majority of it western leaf for use in snuff and cigar wrapper and filler.[6] Finally, Kentucky was now doing a brisk business in rehandling leaf, notably in Western Kentucky, to the tune of some $629,530. Twenty establishments employed 235 people.

One should not let these figures be misleading. While Kentucky was a major tobacco-growing state in 1880, it was a very minor factor in manufactured goods. Total value of all leaf processing and manufacture in Kentucky was $5.3 million, while flour and meal came to $9.6 million, and distilled liquors to $8.3 million, out of total manufactures of $75.5 million. Ten years later, when the state's factory production stood at nearly $127 million, tobacco goods reached a value of $11.3 million ($6.8 million, or about two-thirds, being plug); but whisky was, at $15 million, the leading manufactured product of the state.

5. But Louisville *sold* over 65,000 hogsheads in 1880.
6. Students will find the Tenth Census of 1880 a mine of information on all aspects of leaf cultivation and manufacture. For example, it shows that "colory" lugs were selling for between $7.00 and $9.00 per hundredweight, while "fine leaf" went for $20.00–$24.00. Dark or Red Burley "shipping" leaf, sun- and air-cured filler (for plug), "African" leaf (what is now called "Black Fat"), and leaf for the Regie (European state tobacco monopolies) ranged in price from $2.00 per hundredweight for "poor lugs" to $40.00 for "fine, light wrapper." The heavy, stripped Green River leaf went to England or into domestic "Fine-cut Chewing Tobacco."

In 1890 there were thirty-eight factories in the Commonwealth making chewing and smoking tobaccos, up by ten over 1880, and the value of their output stood at almost $6.8 million, or 75 percent above the figure reached a decade earlier. Louisville remained the dominant manufacturing city with production of $54.5 million, or nearly half the state's total, and her plug goods were valued at $5.1 million. Although there were eleven plants manufacturing chewing and smoking tobaccos in the city, the giant among them was the National Tobacco Works, which alone accounted for 15 percent of the nation's plug. Next to Louisville, Covington was second in leaf products, including chewing and smoking tobaccos worth almost a million dollars, and a quarter-million dollar business in stemming and rehandling. Newport was a distant third, and Lexington failed to report any tobacco manufactures at all.

It was in stemming and rehandling of leaf that the state's greatest progress was made, for the number of such plants was up from twenty in 1880 to seventy-nine in 1890 and the value of their goods had increased almost six times, to nearly $3.5 million. Louisville had sixteen rehandling establishments doing an annual business of about $1.5 million, and there were other large facilities of this sort in the Black Patch region, notably Hopkinsville, Paducah, and Owensboro.

And while the number of cigar and cigarette factories was up from 107 to 144, they seem to have been all small operations, for production increased less than 10 percent over 1880's unimpressive figure. Nationally the facts are that, if plug was enjoying an ever-increasing vogue between 1865 and 1900, the cigar was a no less popular mode of taking tobacco; and sale of cigars and cigarettes (the latter not yet an important item) stood at nearly $130 million in the United States, a figure exactly twice that for chewing, smoking, and snuff manufactures combined, and up from the $9 million total of 1859.

Over 11,000 establishments made cigars, or cigars and cigarettes combined,[7] but the overwhelming concentration of this industry was in New York and Pennsylvania, although Ohio, California, and (increasingly) Florida were important fabricators. While the well-to-do aficionado of Boston, New York, or Philadelphia might then have smoked Havana cigars, the man in the street was much more likely to be puffing on a stogie or some other strong, dark cigar—a "brown roller"—an important constituent of which was wrapper and filler made from the heavy leaf of Western Kentucky.[8]

Nationally, the leaf crop in 1890 was only a little larger than that of 1880 and amounted to 488 million pounds; but Kentucky's harvest leaped 50 million pounds to 221 million, or nearly half the total. No other state was close (see fig. 3). In Kentucky 274,587 acres were sown to tobacco, yielding an average of 809 pounds (better than 100 pounds above the national average) (see fig. 4). Prices were good at 8 to 12 cents a pound. Moreover, the "eastward shift" in Kentucky's

7. In those days, the manufacture of cigars and cigarettes could not by law be carried on in the same factory with chewing and smoking tobaccos.

8. So important was Pennsylvania in the early history of the big black American cigar that the "stogie" was a Pennsylvania invention, its name a contraction of "Conestoga," the wagon that carried western settlers to their new lands, all contentedly puffing stogies most likely made in Philadelphia. The state continues to be a major grower of cigar leaf. In 1890 Lancaster County marketed a level 19 million pounds of leaf, the biggest one-county crop in the country.

Other states that continue to grow significant amounts of cigar leaf include Minnesota, Wisconsin, Florida, Connecticut, and Massachusetts. In the latter two, along the Connecticut River Valley, fine leaf for cigar wrappers is grown under light muslin cover stretched over high frameworks. The most costly of all leaf raised in the United States, Shade-grown tobacco was fetching $4.00 a pound in 1973, when Burley brought a record 93 cents.

leaf cultivation was becoming apparent now. While the "Giants of the West," Christian, Daviess, Graves, Henderson, Logan, Todd, and Webster counties continued to harvest between 7 and 11 million pounds of Dark-fired and Dark Air-cured leaf apiece, the Bluegrass and Northern Kentucky had started to bring in crops of tobacco to be reckoned with. The sectional leader remained Mason County, with 8.2 million pounds; but Bath, Bourbon, Bracken, Fleming, Grant, Harrison, Henry, Owen, Pendleton and Scott counties each had production above 4 million pounds, and Boone, Carroll, Clark, Kenton, Lewis, Montgomery, Nicholas, Shelby, Trimble, and Woodford counties exceeded the 2 million pound mark.

In far more important ways for the nation's tobacco industry, 1890 was a bench-mark year separating two distinct eras in the later history of this commodity and the economy founded upon it. Before that year, the manufacture and sale of tobacco products was largely carried on by thousands of relatively small companies serving a local or regional market, production was largely by hand assisted by a few simple machines like those used to compress and cut plug or twist (cigarettes and cigars were still being rolled, for example, which limited their production and elevated their price), and sales were handled by drummers working directly with retailers. Advertising, where it existed, was confined to a box in a newspaper, a sign in a tobacconist's window, attention-getting brand names, giveaway or coupon-redemption promotional gimmicks, fancy packaging, or point-of-sale inducements like a built-in gas flame cigar lighter with an advertising message. The cigar industry had pioneered fancy packaging and trade names, the latter often with some topical reference or exotic (usually Spanish or Latin American) allusion, in the form of the highly ornamented cigar box and cigar band, and the great breakthrough in point-of-sale promotion, the cigar-store Indian, a large, erect, painted wooden effigy like no human who ever lived, proffering a fistful of wooden cigars to the passerby. Both date from the 1820s.

By 1875 competition in the tobacco industry was rampant on many levels—between East and West, Bright and Burley leaf, chewing, smoking, and cigars, flat plug and fine "navy" cut, even within each class of product such as plug. Indeed, the modern advertising premise of brand identification began among plug manufacturers at about this time, using two main techniques: distinctive (and highly secret) formulas of flavorings and leaf mixtures to achieve identity in taste and brand-name packaging. In the case of plug and twist, brand-name packaging seems to have originated with Lorillard in New York and New Jersey [9] about 1870 with "Tin Tag" brand, so named because each bar of plug or twist bore a brightly colored tin tag an inch or less wide and bent so as to provide a clamp for the tobacco by means of a prong on either end. Along with this new brand-naming and packaging, "Tin Tag" also tied a premium program to the new tags, which could be redeemed by the purchaser for between ⅛ and ½ cent apiece, depending on the size of the package, in exchange for cash or prizes.

Everyone quickly got in on the act, and brand-names and tin tags rapidly proliferated (although the number of manufacturers was gradually contracting into a few giants). Since at the height of this competitive madness there were more than 12,000 brands bidding for the buyer's favor nationally, it would be futile to attempt to enumerate them, but a few of the choicer brands cannot be omitted. Before the era of registered trademarks began in 1885, there were nine plugs named "Legal

9. By 1885 Lorillard's huge Jersey City plant was producing 10 percent of all the nation's manufactured tobacco products. By 1890 only Liggett and Myers's immense Saint Louis works exceeded Lorillard in poundage. Sixteen years later, Lorillard's 25 million pounds of chewing tobaccos was behind both Saint Louis and Louisville; but the Jersey City giant manufactured an additional 14 million pounds of pipe mixtures.

Tender," eleven "Honey Dew," six "Strawberry," four "Pine Apple," and three "Honey Suckle." Other notable trade names included "Grit," "Jaw Bone," "Hard Pan," "Ring Coil Hot Cake," "Sam Jones' Vest Chew," "Mule Ear," and "Susin's Excelsior Tarred Chewing." The National Works at Louisville manufactured "Newsboy," "Lic Quid," and "Monkey Wrench Plug," not to mention the aptly named "Battle Axe," which became a "fighting brand" in the plug wars of the 1890s. Pfingst, Doerhoefer and Company of Louisville registered "Piper Heidsieck," the "gentleman's quid," and thereby set off a local frenzy of naming plugs after French champagnes, leading McNamara, Sealts and Mullen of Covington to respond with "Champagne" and "Mumm's Extra Dry." At about the same time, Harry Weissinger of Louisville, a "navy" manufacturer—i.e., a Burley plug maker of flattened twist as opposed to the flat "Bright" plug of Virginia and North Carolina—introduced to a waiting nation a brand that hit an imaginative high never since equaled, to wit "Prune Nuggets," or lumps of prune flavored and colored Burley chaw, which ran nine to the pound in twelve-pound boxes and sold for the inflated price of 62 cents a pound, when regular plug was selling for 40 cents and "fighting" brands went for as little as 12 or 13 cents. The appeal of "Prune Nuggets" lay in their "novel and attractive shapes" and interesting flavor.

But as the brilliant nationwide advertising and merchandising methods of Blackwell's Durham Tobacco Company (the makers of the still-popular "Bull Durham," a bagged shredded tobacco for pipe or, later, roll-your-own cigarettes) came to be adopted in the tobacco industry generally, the manufacture of leaf products began to be concentrated more and more in the hands of fewer and fewer, larger and larger companies. Completion of a coast-to-coast railroad network made practicable nationwide sales organizations and rapid distribution of manufactured tobacco products from a large central factory. Direct selling to retail outlets on a discount-by-volume-of-sales basis, in addition to national advertising and promotional gimmicks, gave the large companies a great competitive advantage over local manufacturers. This latter was compounded by the growing mechanization of the mass production of leaf products, for the Bonsack Cigarette machine was patented in 1883, making possible the rapid manufacture of cigarettes in huge quantities inexpensively, whereas before they had been hand-rolled at the rate of four or five a minute. Cornering the rights to this machine by W. Duke Sons and Company of North Carolina became the foundation of the mightiest tobacco products empire the nation has ever known. Furthermore, the development of the bag-jack for loading, labeling, and packaging sacks of pipe tobacco like "Bull Durham" made this form of tobacco even more popular. Eventually, bagged tobacco was to supplant plug and twist as the common man's preferred mode of using leaf between 1900 and 1920. More important, it was to pave the way for the rise to domination of the modern cigarette, an event that has revolutionized the industry from top to bottom. Furthermore, the growing popularity of such bagged smoking mixtures as "Bull Durham" forced tobacco manufacturers to diversify their line of products by adding bagged tobacco, which further encouraged concentration of production in a few big firms.

The result of all these changes was that, by 1890–1900, the small quidmaker had all but disappeared and the plug industry was concentrated in the hands of ten large manufacturers who controlled 60 percent of chewing tobacco sales in the United States: Liggett and Myers of Saint Louis, and National in Louisville, each of whom produced 27 million pounds of tobacco products annually, or 14 percent of the national total; Drummond Brothers, and Butler, also of Saint Louis; John Finzer, in Louisville; Sorg, in Middletown, Ohio; Scotten, in Detroit; Lorillard, in Jersey City; and Reynolds and Hanes, in Winston, North Carolina. The western companies together held 52 percent of the national market in plug, the other 8 percent divided between Lorillard and Reynolds.[10]

Unfortunately, the prosperity of these big western plug makers was to prove illusory, for they lacked diversification of products with wide national acceptance that new competitive conditions required for survival. The large New York, New Jersey, Virginia, and North Carolina companies, on the other hand, marketed between them a variety of products. Cigars, snuff, and fine-cut chewing tobacco, for example, were virtually an eastern monopoly; Virginia and North Carolina dominated the trade in bagged smoking tobacco and flat (Bright-leaf) plug and twist; and together all four states had the up-and-coming cigarette trade to themselves. A combination of the seaboard tobacco companies would produce a titan against which the "Giants of the West" could not persevere in any prolonged commercial warfare.

10. Reynolds and Hanes was the forerunner of the modern R. J. Reynolds Tobacco Company, which revolutionized the tobacco industry in 1913 with the introduction of "Camel" cigarettes. Reynolds's inroads into the plug market were considerable: by 1906 Reynolds sold 20 million pounds of Flat (Bright-leaf) Chew, and by 1912 had gained a quarter of the national market.

5

War in the Marketplace and Patch, 1890—1911

THE TREND toward consolidation in the tobacco industry, which had brought the half-dozen or so western plug manufacturers to dominance in that trade, when carried through to its logical end of corporate gigantism, was to spell their extinction. But the warfare in the marketplace that ushered in this great tobacco empire also generated a populist insurrection of Kentucky leaf planters that for a period threatened to reduce the Commonwealth to anarchy.

The opening shot was fired in 1890, when under the guiding hand of J. B. Duke, president of the up-and-coming firm of W. Duke and Sons, a huge combine of the principal eastern tobacco manufacturing companies was put together. Named the American Tobacco Company, it soon came to be called simply the "Trust," for like Rockefeller's Standard Oil and Carnegie's United States Steel its aims were baldly monopolistic. In little more than twenty years, its aims were achieved; and in so doing, the impact of the Trust on Kentucky's leaf economy was shattering. In organizing the Trust, "Buck" Duke created a single monolithic entity out of the five leading tobacco companies of the country: W. Duke and Sons, Allen and Ginter, and F. S. Kinney of Richmond; Goodwin and Company, New York City; and W. S. Kimball and Company, Rochester, New York. Among them, they controlled over 90 percent of the cigarette trade, which Duke, with his unique Bonsack cigarette machine, correctly saw as the wave of the future in the tobacco industry,[1] and were important manufacturers of snuff, flat plug, fine chew, and smoking mixtures. By 1910 the Trust controlled 86.1 percent of American cigarette sales, 84.9 percent of plug, 76.2 percent of smoking tobaccos, 79.7 percent of fine-cut chew, 96.5 percent of snuff, 91.4 percent of little cigars, and 14.4 percent of cigars. Duke's method of achieving his ends was simplicity itself in the day of Robber Barons: his companies simply began ruthless price wars in a single product line in order to drive competitors, not out of business, but into joining the Trust, usually on generous terms. In such wars, a given product line named a "battle brand," the price of which was cut below its cost; and competitors —usually one-product companies—had to respond with "battle brands" of their own, marketed at a competitive price. This meant ruinous losses for all concerned, but profits from other lines more than covered the Trust's losses in the war product, while competitors had no such way of offsetting their deficits and were forced to sell out to Duke. Thus over 250 manufacturers disappeared into the American Tobacco Company or one of its subsidiaries.

Inevitably, the first commercial offensive of Duke and his allies should have been against the upstart western manufacturers of Navy (Burley) cut-plug and twist, their most formidable rivals; and between 1894 and 1898 a mighty "Plug War" raged across tobacconists' counters from coast to coast. Louisville's National To-

1. In 1880, sale of cigarettes in the United States stood at 400 million, as opposed to some 2.4 billion cigars; but by 1888 W. Duke and Sons alone manufactured 744 million cigarettes, or about 40 percent of the national total of over 1.6 billion.

bacco Works responded vigorously and marketed an aptly named plug, "Battle Axe," as a fighting brand. It sold for 13 cents a pound to the trade, although it cost 21 cents a pound to manufacture.[2] They continued their most popular brand, "Newsboy," at its regular price; but profits from that could not cover losses on "Battle Axe." Similarly, Liggett and Myers brought out "Scalping Knife" to do battle while continuing their popular "Star" brand at its regular price; Drummond Brothers did battle with "Crossbow," and Sorg of Middletown entered the lists with "Quality and Quantity." Needless to say, it was all in vain. By the end of 1898 American had secured options on the purchase of all its major competitors except Liggett and Myers, which joined the next year, and organized a sibling, the Continental Tobacco Company, to contain its plug, twist, and fine-cut operations. Into Continental went Louisville's National Tobacco Works and John Finzer; Saint Louis's Drummond Brothers, Brown, Wright Brothers, and James G. Butler; Daniel Scotten, Detroit; P. T. Sorg of Middletown; and J. Wright and P. H. Mayo of Richmond. The biggest prize of all, next to Liggett, was Lorillard and Sons, which also fell into the Continental net in 1898; and in 1899 Continental gained control of R. J. Reynolds, an important plug and smoking manufacturer. All that remained in the plug war were mopping-up operations.

With the acquisition of Lorillard, American gained a bridgehead in the snuff trade; and in 1899–1900 a furious if short-lived "snuff war" was fought, which ended in the capitulation of George W. Helme, a leading independent, and the organization of another parasite concern, the American Snuff Company. Other commercial wars followed, including the organization of the Consolidated Tobacco Company to invade England and

2. The leaf alone cost 6 cents a pound, and taxes added another 7 cents.

foreign markets, which established a beachhead; but the battle was a draw, and a new détente of the contending parties emerged, called the British-American Tobacco Company, Limited, which still exists. In 1901–1902 the American Cigar Company was organized in order to prosecute aggression on a new front—the "cigar war"—with limited success, for cigar-making remains a hand operation among innumerable relatively small firms who enjoy great customer loyalty to their products. Nevertheless, American picked up a cigar operation in Kentucky which is still turning out a plentiful supply of "Roi-Tan" cigars.

While all this moving and shaking was taking place in the halls of the commercial mighty, and Kentucky's tobacco manufacturing industry was being gobbled up by the colossus of the East, things were going badly in the Black Patch, and the farmers there were getting into a decidedly ugly mood. The reason was simple enough: tobacco prices were falling sharply in Western Kentucky, so that by 1904 they had reached a point that was unendurable for the planters. The three main grades of ' leaf were bringing 3, 2, and 1 cents a pound, respectively, where before, earlier in the 1890s, prices had ranged between 8 and 12 cents for the medium to better grades.

A number of factors were at work together to bring about this depression in leaf prices. National production of leaf had nearly doubled between 1889 and 1899, from 488 million to 868 million pounds, and reached 1.05 billion by 1909. Formidable competitors closer to manufacturing centers were also increasing production, like North Carolina, whose leaf crop quadrupled between 1889 and 1899, from 36 to 127.5 million pounds, and Virginia, whose production almost tripled during the same period (48.5 to 123 million pounds). Kentucky's crop reached 314 million pounds, up from 221.8 million ten years before; but much of this was not of good quality, for marginal leaf was beginning to reach the market in substantial quantities and driving down the price. Furthermore the pitiless warfare between the "Trust" and the "Independents" for the market in chewing tobaccos reduced profits so radically that only minimal prices could be paid for plug leaf—and that meant Black Patch leaf. Foreign demand for dark leaf was also falling off during the same period, which had theretofore accounted for a third of Western leaf production. Changing tastes at home away from plug and toward cigarettes, pipe mixtures, and lighter, milder cigars,[3] in which the various strains of Black Patch leaf—"One-sucker," "Shoestring," "Morrow," "Blue" and "Yellow" Pryor, Henderson Dark-fired, and the rest—played a minor role or none at all, further slackened interest in "Western Red Burley" (see fig. 5).

Then too, marketing procedures for leaf tobacco were undergoing radical changes, and tobacco farmers were slow to adjust to altering conditions at the point of sale, which was for them, after all, a matter of economic life or death. More and more western tobacco was bought loose, rather than prized into a hogshead, at "the barn door." A lot of "chute buying" was also done: planters' wagons were driven into a roofed driveway with a loading platform on which the buyers stood and bid on wagon loads. In Owensboro, Green River tobacco was still being sold in hogsheads, with bidding going on over sample leaf "hands" that had been broken out by an inspector. Further east, Louisville's big hogshead market on Main Street was strong and by 1900 was handling 175,000 hogsheads. By 1904, however, Charles Bohmer introduced in Lexington a revolutionary new system of loose-leaf auction in graded baskets or trays of several hundred pounds each, a practice which had been introduced in Virginia a few years earlier and had proved popular with both buyers and growers because of increased quality control and, for the good farmer at

3. The latter a product of the Spanish-American War.

least, better prices. The effect of this change in marketing over the next half-century, together with the development of cheap farm trucks and a network of farm-to-market roads, was entirely to eliminate hogshead sales of tobacco (and with it Louisville as a major leaf market) and to bring Lexington, followed rather distantly by Maysville, Carrollton, and Shelbyville, to preeminence as loose-leaf auction markets and as warehouse and re-handling centers (see fig. 6).

Finally, in June 1898, Congress levied an oppressive new tax of $1.50 per thousand on all cigarettes, and 12 cents a pound on other manufactured tobacco products, which radically increased the cost to the consumer, and, in the case of cigarettes, cut back demand for a decade. Although the tax was reduced in 1902 to 54 cents per thousand on cigarettes wholesaling at $2.00 a thousand, to $1.08 per thousand on cigarettes wholesaling above $2.00 a thousand, and to 6 cents a pound on other manufactured tobacco products, leaf prices remained depressed during these years of very large crops.

Whatever the real reasons for the decline in tobacco prices to the disastrous "3-2-1" levels of the early 1900s, Western Kentucky planters blamed it on the diabolical machinations of the fabulously wealthy "Trust," the British-based Imperial Tobacco Company, and the European state tobacco monopolies called the "Regie," whose buyers, they felt, were conspiring deliberately to keep the cost of leaf at the lowest possible figure in order to enhance their already swollen profits. There may have been some truth to this suspicion, although it was never proved; but the problems in the marketplace outlined above would have been more than sufficient to account for low leaf prices. However that may be, Black Patch leaf growers saw their Dr. Fell in the Trust and the Regie, particularly as these remote and anonymous entities were personified by their local representatives, the leaf buyers and warehousemen. And in a time of militant populist unrest in all rural areas, a mass meet-

87

ing of disaffected dark tobacco planters was called. On Sunday, September 24, 1904, some 5,000 persons gathered at the fairgrounds in Guthrie, Todd County, Kentucky, for a barbecue, some speechifying, and no doubt a little hunkering.[4] Out of all the rhetoric and pork fat an association was formed which eventually came to be called the Dark-fired Tobacco District Planters' Protective Association of Kentucky and Tennessee, Incorporated—or generally "The Association"—the aim of which was to force tobacco prices up to an acceptable level, 8 cents a pound being the immediate goal.

To achieve this end, the Association proposed to form a cooperative that would monopolize the sale of Black Patch leaf (which comprised about half the nation's total production) and hold it off the market until an acceptable price was realized. To do this required that an overwhelming majority of the planters join the Association and agree to sell their leaf only through that organization. Altogether, about 70 percent of the Black Patch growers joined at the height of the movement, and enough shares were sold in the Association to buy warehouses, set up a marketing center in Clarksville, Tennessee, establish a headquarters in Guthrie, and offer cash advances on the first year's crop of 25–50 percent. Sympathetic merchants and professional people, whose livelihood depended upon the fortunes of the planters, also joined in large numbers; and optimism about the prospects of success for this populist revolt ran high as tobacco poured into the Association's warehouses all over the Black Patch.

There were, however, two inherent weaknesses in the Association's strategy, sound and even daring as it was. To be successful, a much larger percentage of growers than the 70 percent that was achieved would be necessary in order to force the price of leaf up to the target

4. Hunkering: squatting down on one's haunches and drinking whisky, preferably moonshine.

figure. Because it was a voluntary cooperative, there were no legal means to compel the notoriously independent Black Patch planters to join, nor to make them market their leaf through the Association exclusively. Finally, because the Association lacked the enormous financial resources of the "Trust," "Regie," and Imperial buyers, who could pay cash on the hogshead for all the leaf they bought, it could only offer a small cash advance on a farmer's crop delivered to one of its warehouses, with a chancy prospect of full payment as much as six months away. To Western Kentucky planters perennially in hock to local merchants for seed, equipment, and supplies, such a delay in payment, with no certainty of an advantageous sale at the end, constituted a real hardship and a desperate gamble. That 70 percent signed up is testimony to their courage as well as to their desperation.

Needless to say, the great monopolists, who were old hands at economic infighting, saw at once the weakness in the Association's position and moved quickly to exploit it, offering through their buyers to purchase leaf grown by independent planters at prices ranging up to 12 cents a pound, with the clear intention of attempting to break the Association's ranks. The strategy did not work. In May 1905, Felix G. Ewing, the Association's capable general manager and all-round wheelhorse, sold 5,000 hogsheads of members' leaf to George Reussens, of New York, for the European market, and shortly thereafter disposed of the rest of the crop of 24,700 hogsheads (between 25 and 33 million pounds) for an average of 6.66 cents a pound, and the great aims of the organization seemed close to realization.[5] Nevertheless,

5. From the start the Association attracted vigorous leaders, eloquent orators, gifted organizers, and effective spokesmen in legislative chambers, including Charles H. and Joel Fort, John M. Foster, Charles E. Baker, Frank Walton, E. T. Bondurant, Col. John B. Allen, Bob Taylor, Congressman Ollie James of Marion, Kentucky, Congressman Will Fowler of Nashville,

the weaknesses in the Association which were eventually to prove fatal remained beneath the veneer of apparent victory over their powerful international array of enemies.

On September 23, 1905, the Association held its second mass rally, barbecue, and oratorical display at the fairgrounds in Guthrie, to which some 18,000 persons came, representing 7,000 members in twenty-eight Western Kentucky and Tennessee counties. Trust and Regie buyers continued to lure independents with offers of 8–12 cents a pound, but Ewing managed to sell the Association's 1905 crop at good prices, including one order of 6,000 hogsheads from the Italian Regie at 9 cents a pound. A sister organization, the Virginia Dark Tobacco Association, was organized with three-year membership pledges. The growers' cooperative idea seemed to be developing into a national movement with quite revolutionary possibilities of making the farmer's voice a force to be reckoned with in the land. By 1906, on a short crop, Dark-fired leaf marketed through the Association reached an average price of 7.33 cents a pound, memberships climbed to 12,000, and fully 25,000 turned out for the annual festivities at the Guthrie fairgrounds, where Congressman A. O. Stanley, among others, spoke. On this occasion, the banner of the Association was unfurled, a golden tobacco leaf on a ground of purest white, signifying the chaste motives of the membership, and, presumably, their desire for lucre.

Unfortunately, somewhat less pure motives were

George Snadon, Dr. David Alfred Amoss, C. P. Warfield, C. E. Barker, R. E. Cooper, and A. O. Stanley, congressman and later senator and governor, an able and level-headed advocate of the planters who fought long and successfully against powerful lobbying interests for economic relief. Felix "King" Ewing, general manager of the Association, was himself a wealthy planter with over 3,000 acres in Robertson County, Tennessee.

working within this cooperative organization, directed against that recalcitrant hard core of independents (contemptuously called "hillbillies" by the membership) who had refused to join and continued to sell "bootleg leaf" to the Trust and Regie buyers, often at inflated prices. Early in October 1906, thirty-two Association members met secretly at Stainback Schoolhouse, near Felix Ewing's farm in Robertson County, Tennessee, and organized a clandestine movement within the Association determined to cow the independent hillbillies into joining the organization by intimidation and, if necessary, by violence. Direct action against buyers, warehouses, factories, and rehandling facilities of the Trust, Imperial, and the Regie was also contemplated.

Initially named "Possum Hunters," the movement spread like wildfire through the Black Patch and was eventually organized as the "Secret Society," along the lines already laid down by the Ku Klux Klan, Masons, and Odd Fellows and replete with robes and masks, an elaborate paramilitary hierarchy operating as an outlaw underground army, awesome ceremonials and rituals of initiation, blood-oaths, secret passwords, handshakes, and signals—in short the whole mumbo jumbo of any subversive protest movement. In a speech at Springfield, Tennessee, late in 1906, A. O. Stanley denounced the just-then emerging insurgent organization and branded it with the name that it was to carry into history, if not infamy: the "night riders." For such they were, masked, hooded, and robed, organized in troops of armed and mounted cavalry who moved by night. They coerced reluctant leaf planters to join the Association, drove other recalcitrants to sell out and flee the state, flogged still others, dragged plant beds, burned barns and houses, killed some, and generally maintained a reign of terror over the Black Patch for over two years, between 1906 and 1908, that finally took the form of full-fledged guerrilla action against entire cities.

It is now generally acknowledged that the leadership

of this well-organized insurgent movement was taken by one of the important figures in the Association, David Amoss, a country doctor and planter of Cobb, Caldwell County, Kentucky, with a military-school background, who at forty-nine was a rugged, solid, and determined man, austere and, in his own quiet way, arrogant and uncompromising—as well as being a first-rate guerrilla leader. He was also a close friend of "King" Ewing and most of the leaders of the Association, who either connived at, or winked at, the campaign of terror so adroitly orchestrated by Amoss and his associates: Guy Dunning, an important planter, Centre College graduate, and Association leaf inspector; Colonel W. H. Malone, also of Caldwell County, along with John W. Hollowell, and Sam Cash, the sheriff of Lyon County, among others, many of whom were veterans of the Civil War and thoroughly experienced in military operations.

A number of factories and warehouses belonging to agents of the Trust and the Regie were either dynamited or burned (or both), or their buyers threatened, during December 1906, culminating in a raid on Princeton, Caldwell County, on the night of December 1, 1906, by a force of 250 heavily armed, masked riders. Striking without warning but with beautiful coordination, separate squads sealed off the roads to Eddyville, Fredonia, and Dawson's Springs, disarmed the police, captured the courthouse, Fire Department, and telephone and telegraph offices, and cut off the water supply. With kerosene and dynamite another squad demolished two Trust and Regie factories containing over 300,000 pounds of leaf. The entire occupation of the town of 1,000 lasted little more than an hour (12:30 to 1:30 A.M.), no one was injured, and the raiders disappeared without trace into the hinterland.

The attack on Princeton established the pattern for such operations. A year later almost to the day, Hopkinsville, a major Trust and Regie warehouse and factory center, was occupied by four columns of mounted men who put the torch to a factory and a warehouse and destroyed some $250,000 of tobacco, beat a Trust leaf buyer, and wrecked the offices of a newspaper critical of the night riders, and then disappeared into the night. The next month, on January 3, 1908, an identical raid on Russellville destroyed two more warehouses of the Trust, one of them owned by the American Snuff Company, and losses reached well beyond $100,000.

Worse yet, the violence was spreading into the White Burley country of Central and Northern Kentucky. A Burley Tobacco Society was organized in 1907, which at its peak counted 35,000 members, and in the fall of 1907 a huge rally of leaf planters at Shelbyville cheered Joel Fort's cry, "No crop for 1908!" Burning and dynamiting followed all across the Bluegrass—in Carroll, Bath, Fleming, Bracken, Kenton, Owen, and Mason counties, even Brown County, Ohio—and accounted for at least 1 million pounds of leaf destroyed in Trust and Regie factories and warehouses; and the loss in buildings came to an additional $500,000.

Forces were at work, however, that would quash the night-rider movement, which had by now reached the dimensions of insurrection. Although in the heart of the Black Patch it was impossible to get a grand jury to indict or a jury to convict a "rider," public opinion was turning against the Association, led by thundering denunciations of the violence and lawlessness of the "Society" by Henry Watterson in the *Louisville Courier-Journal,* by the *Memphis Commercial Appeal,* and even by home-town weeklies in the Patch itself. Newly elected Kentucky Governor Augustus Willson, who ran on a law-and-order platform, called out the militia in Western Kentucky in December 1907, after the Hopkinsville raid, and more companies were activated in January 1908, following the attack on Russellville. A statewide Law and Order League was organized by Mayor Charles M. Meacham of Hopkinsville to resist violence, and a mass rally was held in McCauley's Theater, Louisville, in 1908 to denounce the spreading lawlessness and to consider ways of countering it. A number of charismatic figures were present to lend their support to the League, including the much-revered Confederate general and hero of Fort Donelson, Simon Bolivar Buckner, Governor Willson, and Judge James B. Gregory. Then too, the 1907 tobacco crop was a short one, in part at least caused by night-rider terrorist tactics and plant bed scraping, and the price of leaf climbed to 8 cents a pound, the target-figure of the Association's organizers back in 1904.[6] With this goal reached, some of the Association's cohesiveness began to ebb away and the ranks thinned. And in April 1909 A. O. Stanley finally got the hated tax on tobacco repealed in a rider to the Payne-Aldrich Tariff Act, thereby removing another unifying force for the movement.

Perhaps most important of all, a brilliant young lawyer, John G. Miller of Paducah, took a damage suit against some three dozen night riders filed by one Mary Lou Hollowell and her husband, both holdouts from the Association, who had been visited in the night and beaten by a gang of their neighbors. Unfortunately for the riders, Mary Lou Hollowell was not only an indomitable woman who refused to be intimidated by nightrider threats against her life, but she also had an unerring memory for faces and could identify every one of the gang of ruffians who had attacked her and her husband. Miller, the Hollowell's attorney, intelligently got the case tried before a federal court, where the usual subornation of witnesses and jurors which had worked to exonerate accused night riders in local courts would

6. The Association's ten major warehouses in Paducah, Clarksville, Hopkinsville, Russellville, Princeton, Murray, Guthrie, and Cadiz sold 39,000 hogsheads of leaf for $5.5 million in this year, which marked the high tide of the "Society of Equity."

count for little. After one jury was hung, a second trial in May 1908 resulted in a guilty verdict against the culprits and an award of $35,000 in damages, which Guy Dunning, Amoss's chief lieutenant, was eventually to settle for $15,000.

Damage suits brought against the night riders by their victims proliferated following the Hollowell verdict, at one point totaling almost a quarter-million dollars; convictions and heavy awards of claims were delivered, and many of the riders were ruined, forced to flee, or had to hide out. The back of this terrorist organization was broken, once the hooded riders realized that they could be held accountable before the law for their acts, and the Secret Society simply dissolved. By Christmas 1908 the last of the troopers occupying Western Kentucky were withdrawn, and the end of the Black Patch War was at hand, although the Association lingered on until 1915 as a leaf cooperative.

Meanwhile, other legal actions were afoot on the national scene that were contributing to the dissolution of the Association and were to have profound effects not only on Kentucky but on the entire tobacco industry. For by a ruling of the United States Supreme Court handed down on May 29, 1911—a decision upholding a 1908 ruling of the Federal Court of Appeals for the Southern District of New York State—the great American Tobacco combine was declared to be in violation of the Sherman Anti-Trust Act of 1890—a law enacted, ironically enough, in the same year that J. B. Duke put together the Trust which was from the outset so clearly in violation of the letter and spirit of that law. Furthermore, the Court ordered Duke to prepare a plan for partition of the great structure, naming some thirty-two companies and twenty-nine individual officers as the offenders in a conspiracy to restrain, i.e., monopolize, trade in leaf products. Duke's plan, which was submitted to and accepted by the court and Attorney General Wickersham on November 16, 1911, created a number of new companies out of the old monolith, none of which alone could monopolize the production and sale of tobacco products as the parent company had done to the detriment of real competition in the industry.

The effect of the ruling was to create the American tobacco industry as it is today. Only very recent developments have altered the structure of the industry laid down by the court in 1911. In any event, the court's action did away with a monopolistic organization only to substitute for it an oligopolistic structure of a few large tobacco manufacturers, whose domination of the industry has been (with two exceptions of particular interest to Kentuckians) as great as that of the Old Trust and just as inimical to the growth of incipient competitors.

Still, the dissolution of the Trust removed the last shibboleth which had served to rally planters around the stainless banner of the Association; and with Burley prices in 1911 ranging between 9 and 12 cents a pound, the raison d'être of the movement had vanished.

6

Making the Modern Tobacco Industry, 1911—1939

W<small>HAT EMERGED</small> from the partition of the Trust, once the United Cigar Company, the Imperial Tobacco Company, British-American, and other holdings were separately divested, were four large concerns—the "Big Four," as they came to be called. With assets of $98.4 million, the biggest was the American Tobacco Company, whose strength was in cigarettes, smoking tobacco, and plug; Liggett and Myers, at $67.4 million, was well diversified, as was Lorillard, with $47.6 million. By far the smallest of the "Big Four" at the outset was R. J. Reynolds, the bulk of whose assets was in flat Bright-leaf cut plug, with no cigarette products to speak of.

In order to strengthen their competitive position vis-à-vis the three giants, Reynolds's management astutely judged that broadening their product line into the increasingly popular cigarette field would be the best tactic. But to succeed, any new brand of cigarette would have to be dramatically different from anything then on the market, and it would need to be massively advertised and promoted in order to gain the brand-name recognition nationally that "Bull Durham" had demonstrated thirty years before. Correctly guessing that the trend in tobacco tastes was toward greater mildness, Reynolds boldly developed a wholly new kind of blended cigarette employing together all the leaf strains enjoyed separately in existing cigarette brands. Thus "Turkish" leaf was added for flavor to a base of Virginia and North Carolina Bright-leaf; and to this mixture— taking a cue from the manufacturers of pipe mixtures and Navy cut plug—was added about 30 percent Kentucky White Burley, which had the unique property among tobaccos of absorbing and holding the heavy load of sweeteners and flavorings that Reynolds planned for the taste of this new blended cigarette. A little later, a modicum of Maryland leaf was added to improve the burning qualities of the blend.

With that, the formula of the modern American blended cigarette was set, and it has remained largely unchanged down to the present day. The brand name "Camel" was given to it, with a picture of a dromedary on the package placed in a suitably Egyptian setting to capitalize on the popular preference for "Turkish" cigarettes just then. Reynolds marketed the new brand in a new and seductive manner—in packs of twenty cigarettes selling for a dime, at a time when such packaging was associated in the popular mind with relatively more expensive "class" brands like "Fatima," which sold for 15 cents. Finally, Reynolds shrewdly played the advertising toward a hitherto untapped market larger than the existing one: women; and the female emancipation ushered in by World War I and the "Roaring Twenties" played into the "Camel" hand as though they had been arranged by the advertising agency. The upshot was that "Camel," introduced in the Cleveland marketing area in 1913, caught on at once. By 1915 it had carried off 20 percent of the nation's cigarette sales; by 1918–1919, it had 40 percent; by 1922, 45 percent.

The other companies were slow to grasp the revolution Reynolds had singlehandedly effected, and it was not until 1918 that American grabbed the name off Patterson's chewing tobacco, "Lucky Strike" (which dated back to the 1850s), and gave it to their own blended cigarette. By 1924 "Luckies" had 16 percent of national cigarette sales, and eventually became the chief rival of "Camel," although it exceeded the latter's annual sales only once. Liggett and Myers, slower yet in responding to the Reynolds challenge, did not introduce "Chesterfield" until 1919, but by 1925 they held 25 percent of the market. Last of all, Lorillard introduced "Old Gold" in 1926, but it never really caught on, and by 1949 could command no more than 5.1 percent of national sales, whereas by 1925 "Camel," "Lucky Strike," and "Chesterfield" accounted for 82.3 percent of the vastly increased national sale of what had now become the dominant form of tobacco consumption, the cigarette.

In order to comprehend the profound impact on Kentucky's tobacco economy effected by the brilliant success of the modern blended cigarette in 1913 and the positive stampede of smokers and former nonsmokers to the cigarette (particularly women) during the intervening years, some explanation is necessary. The Dark-fired and Dark Air-cured leaf grown in the Black Patch since Civil War days had been principally employed in the manufacture of snuff, Burley plug, and "brown-rolled" cigars or stogies, consumption of which had begun to decline by 1920. Smoking tobacco mixtures, which used no Western Kentucky dark leaf, held their own until the onset of World War II, after which they too slipped into relative insignificance where they remain today (see fig. 5).

The only growth in the tobacco industry over the last two generations has been in cigarette consumption, a product in which dark tobaccos figure not at all. Indeed, even earlier, cigarettes had ignored Western dark leaf, whether "all domestic"—i.e., "Virginia Bright"—as in "Piedmont," "Sweet Caporal," or "Home Run," and most modern English and Canadian cigarettes, such as

"Players"; or "Turkish"—i.e., pseudo-"Turkish," a half-and-half mixture of Bright and Near Eastern leaf—as in "Hassan," "Mecca," or "Murad," and many still popular European brands which came into brief popular favor between 1900 and 1920 (see fig. 6).

At the same time, the need for White Burley as a flavoring vehicle in pipe mixtures, chewing tobaccos, and the increasingly important blended cigarette, brought it into greater and greater demand, and stimulated its cultivation in Kentucky—and particularly in the northern, central, and southwest-central counties—while the production of Western Kentucky dark leaf was enduring an equally spectacular decline. Today, Kentucky dark-leaf production of all sorts is about 20 million pounds a year, while White Burley, depending on growing conditions, ranges between 350 and 550 million pounds (see fig. 4). By the same token, prices for White Burley leaf, because it has come to be in greater demand in what is now a cigarette tobacco economy, has consistently fetched higher prices than dark leaf, and by 1973 was widening the margin dramatically, when it averaged over $93 per hundredweight (see fig. 8). What this change has meant consists in this: nowadays, the forty-eight tobacco-growing counties of Central Kentucky harvest about two-thirds of the state's total leaf crop (see figs. 4, 10, 11, and 12).

A glance at figure 6 should demonstrate this domination of the state's trade in leaf by White Burley, which now jockeys for preeminence even in the Black Patch with One-Sucker, Green River, and Eastern and Western Dark-fired, and has indeed reduced their areas of cultivation to islands in a sea of Burley which has spilled over into southern Ohio and Indiana, West Virginia, western Virginia and North Carolina, and Tennessee (see also fig. 2).

Throughout these years, the consumption of tobacco products was increasing by leaps and bounds, and to keep pace leaf production was expanding at an enormous rate. At 868 million pounds in 1899, the national crop of tobacco was nearly twice that of ten years before; by 1909 it exceeded 1 billion pounds, and in the record year of 1919—the first year after World War I had ended—over 1.37 billion pounds was harvested, and White Burley was bringing the unheard-of figure of 34 cents a pound, up from 12.7 cents in 1916. By 1909 Kentucky grew almost 400 million pounds of leaf worth nearly $40 million, and the 1916 crop of 462 million pounds netted the state's planters $58.67 million. Three years later, poundage exceeded 506 million from 634,038 acres (or nearly twice the 1899 total of 384,805 acres) and averaged just under 800 pounds an acre.[1] Tobacco continued to be the state's second most valuable crop, after cereal grains, and accounted for about a third of the state's total farm crop value. In terms of hard cash for the farmer, tobacco was even more important, for much of the crop in grains went for livestock feed and whisky. Thus in the banner year of 1919 leaf sold for $116.4 million, just behind corn ($125 million), and accounted for almost exactly a third of the state's total income from all crops of $347.3 million.

National consumption of manufactured tobacco products continued to climb rapidly during these years. At $316.7 million in 1909, the value of the nation's leaf goods was up 45 percent over 1900 and was to climb to nearly $500 million by 1914 before doubling again to just over $1 billion in 1919. Of the huge increase between 1914 and 1919, nearly all of it was in cigarettes, and better than 75 percent of the value of all tobacco products was shared by cigarettes and cigars. Kentucky's share of these boom years for the tobacco industry unfortunately did not increase. By 1900 the

1. In 1919, some 287,000 acres were sown to White Burley, about 40 percent of the total, and yielded over 241 million pounds, or nearly half the total. Production averaged 840 pounds per acre, well above the state's average for all types.

state's industry produced $22 million in leaf products, or twice the 1890 figure, about 70 percent in chewing and smoking products and a quarter from stemming and rehandling operations. Ominously for Kentucky's long-term future as a manufacturing center, however, cigar and cigarette manufactures comprised only about 7 percent of the total. By 1904 manufactures actually decreased by $2 million, to $15 million (not counting rehandling), but had recovered to $18.6 million by 1909 and reached $24.1 million by 1919. From these figures it is apparent that Kentucky's tobacco products industry, because of its concentration on plug (sales of which had leveled out between 1910 and 1920), was not sharing in the skyrocketing climb of cigarette sales that was carrying the industry nationally to new highs.[2] Worse yet, after 1920 the demand for chewing tobacco began a steady decline to its present relative insignificance. Of the 1919 total of $24.1 million, $20.6 million was concentrated in Louisville, followed by Covington with $1.2 million. The big leaf stemming and rehandling centers continued to be Daviess and McCracken counties, with Christian, Graves, and Henderson counties well back.

The Kentucky leaf crop of 1920 was again very large but of poor quality, for the growing season had been a rainy one, with the result that prices plummeted from the unprecedented high of 34 cents the previous year to 13.4 cents a pound. Angry planters closed the Lexington auction market the second day of sales in protest against the low prices, although the truth is that they had sim-

2. By comparison, North Carolina's tobacco manufactures leaped from $9.5 million in 1899 to almost $260 million in 1919, of which $226 million was in cigarettes. Between 1914 and 1919 New York's production rose from $88 to $166 million, Pennsylvania's from $54 to $104 million, and Virginia's from about $33 to over $78 million. Florida's cigar industry doubled to $38 million in the same period.

ply returned to pre-1919 levels.[3] Nevertheless, violence occurred in spots, and the specter of a revival of the Association and the night riders arose. Next year was even worse: the White Burley crop of 176.6 million pounds was down 40 percent from 1920, although the price had risen to 22.2 cents a pound.

Under these extremely difficult circumstances for leaf planters, credit for preventing a return to the lawlessness of earlier times can be given to the organization of a new pooling arrangement among Burley farmers, the Burley Tobacco Growers Cooperative Association, which had a steadying influence on the desperate tobacconists. The movement to revive the old, moribund Burley Association and to make of it a modern cooperative marketing body was inspired by Robert Worth Bingham, owner of the *Louisville Courier-Journal* and *Times* and a power in national public life and journalism, together with Arthur Krock, a mountain boy who had risen to the editorship of Bingham's *Louisville Times*.[4] Reacting quickly and intelligently to the plight of the Burley growers, Bingham organized a committee to study the problem and recommend a solution. The committee was composed of Bernard Baruch, the New York financier and confidant of presidents and statesmen; Congressman J. C. Cantrill; Krock; Ralph M. Barker, prominent Carrollton warehouseman and a powerful figure in national tobacco circles; Samuel H. Halley, a no less well-known Lexington planter and warehouseman; and John H. Newman of Woodford County, president of the Bur-

3. Other states in the tobacco belt had also disastrously overplanted in the 1920 crop year and had experienced similarly bad weather during the growing and curing season, so that they too marketed a large crop of indifferent leaf and suffered comparable losses.

4. Krock's memoirs, *Myself When Young* (New York, 1973), chronicle these years in a fine evocation of the Louisville ambiance. He glosses over his part in these important events.

ley Association. In meetings in New York the group discussed the situation in Kentucky and determined that the formation of a cooperative pooling and marketing association like that which had succeeded so well for the California fruit growers ought to work as well for Burley planters. The brilliant legal counsel for the California Cooperative, Aaron Sapiro, was brought East to plan and set up a Burley Pool under a resuscitated Burley Association.

An executive committee headed by James C. Stone of Lexington and with as members Barker, William F. Simms of Spring Station, and John T. Collins of Paris (later N. Kehoe) was set up; and Joseph Rossaneau, of Spokane, Washington, an experienced cooperative executive, was hired to organize the Association and its pool. Its goal was to enlist in membership at least 75 percent of Burley growers (including those in Ohio, Indiana, and West Virginia as well as Kentucky) by November 15, 1921, thereby ensuring control of that year's crop when marketed. Most important of all, a new feature required members to pledge themselves to market all their Burley leaf for the next five years through the Association exclusively.

Recruiting went well from the start, and by the time of its organization the Association had 57,000 members with leaf worth more than $50 million, well in excess of the goals set initially. The problem of limited cash reserves with which to purchase warehouses and rehandling facilities and to provide advances to farmers to tide them over the period until the pooled tobacco could be sold to manufacturers—one of the greatest weaknesses of the old Dark-fired Association—was largely (but not completely) solved when substantial funds were raised. Judge Bingham pledged $1 million personally; James B. Brown, president of the National Bank of Kentucky, pledged $500,000; Monte Goble, president of the Fifth-Third National Bank of Cincinnati, put up $1.5 million, and arrangements were made with the War Finance Corporation (of which "Jim" Brown was a director) to advance $10 million once the crop was warehoused.

There was little the new Burley Cooperative could do about the 1921 crop year, which was disastrous for the smaller leaf planters particularly.[5] Nevertheless, of a Burley crop that was greatly reduced from 1920's yield of 297 million pounds to 176.6 million, better than two-thirds (119 million pounds) was delivered to the Burley Association's warehouses. The next year, production stood at 284 million pounds, of which almost 200 million was marketed through the Burley Pool and brought 28.4 cents a pound. In 1923 production hit 354 million pounds (245 million of which went through the Pool) at an average price of 21 cents, which held the next year; but compliance with the Cooperative Association's pledge was softening, and in 1924 only about 60 percent of the crop was marketed through the Pool. The following year, more leaf was sold at public auction than was sent into the Pool; and in 1926, when prices slipped to 12.55 cents a pound (13.25 cents at the Cooperative), Association members failed to renew their pledges for another five-year period. Thus a second great venture in intelligent leaf marketing had come a cropper, and the planter was once again at the mercy of the auction buyer.

The failure of this experiment was largely attributable to leaf growers' reluctance to wait to receive the full value of their crop for as long as it was necessary for the Pool to sell the tobacco. Nevertheless, important lessons for the future were learned. For one, the value of limiting acreage and production vis-à-vis price was clearly established; for the Pool, together with the State Department of Agriculture and the University of Kentucky's School of Agriculture and corps of county

5. One small planter, who had netted $325.00 for his 1919 crop, came away in 1921 with just $2.75.

agents, had encouraged voluntary reduction of over-planting to marginal land, with the result that tobacco acreage averaged about two-thirds of that in 1919, and prices generally reflected these sound management principles. The experience of the short-lived Coopera-tive also demonstrated that any future pooling arrange-ment, to be successful, would require capitalization suf-ficient to insure direct payment to the planter upon receipt of sale; and that kind of money clearly pointed to some federally supported program like that which is presently in being. Finally, the Burley Tobacco Growers Cooperative Association maintained its cor-porate structure and its properties after its practical dis-solution as a cooperative in 1926, so that it stood ready to assume the role of intermediary between government and leaf grower in price-support and acreage-limitation programs beginning in 1941, and remains so today. A comparable body, the Dark-fired Tobacco Growers Co-operative Association, performs similar functions for Western Kentucky leaf planters. All this, however, had to await the coming of the New Deal.

By 1926 Kentucky was beginning to recover the ground it had lost since 1890 as a tobacco manufacturing state. The number of factories had been radically re-duced to a total of seventy-eight, reflecting a nationwide trend toward the bigness required by this pioneer in in-dustrial mechanization and automation, together with a concomitant reduction in the labor force. Statewide, to-bacco manufactures, at $57.3 million, ranked fourth be-hind food products ($109 million), metals ($94 million), and lumber ($65 million). Of this total, almost $36 mil-lion was in cigarettes and chewing tobaccos, $15 million in stemming and rehandling, and $6 million in cigars, altogether employing some 8,385 workers, a dispropor-tionate number of whom were engaged in the relatively unprofitable cigar and rehandling industries. Only 3,004 made cigarettes and plug.

Louisville continued to dominate the industry in Kentucky, employing over 5,700 workers, or nearly 70 percent of the total; and companies incorporated elsewhere had the lion's share of the Louisville and Kentucky production. Thus the two American Tobacco Company plants making plug and pipe tobacco in Louisville employed over 1,100 workers (the last of these was closed down in 1970), followed by a Liggett and Myers stemming and rehandling plant with 977 employees (since closed), and the South Western Tobacco Company rehandling plant at Ninth and Main streets, in the old leaf district, which had 500 workers. R. J. Reynolds's plug and smoking tobacco factory employed 335, just ahead of Eitel and Cassebohm, cigar manufacturers, at 295 (both long since gone); Lorillard's general-purpose factory for tobacco products, with 265; and E. J. O'Brien's rehandling plant at a level of 200 workers (the latter two in business at the time of writing). Two other important manufacturers whose future was to be bright remain to be mentioned, the Axton-Fisher Tobacco Company, manufacturers of chewing and smoking tobaccos and cigarettes, with 210 employees, and the Brown and Williamson Tobacco Corporation, with 180 employees.[6]

There were innumerable independent cigar manufacturers in Louisville and the rest of Kentucky in 1926, almost all of which have since disappeared, but the American Cigar Company (a division of the American Tobacco Company) had three sizable plants in Kentucky, the smallest in Louisville (163 employees), another with 333 employees in Paducah, and the largest of all at 411 workers in Owensboro, which still annually produced some 665 million "Roi-Tan" cigars as of 1965. Important manufacturers included C. F. Vaughan, a leaf wholesaler and rehandler in Fayette and Boyle coun-

6. In 1929 Brown and Williamson built a big new plant in Louisville and moved its general offices there, where they remain. Brown and Williamson is the only major tobacco manufacturer whose headquarters are in Kentucky.

ties, with a total of 345 employees (still doing business as a warehouseman); The Hodge Tobacco Company, a wholesaler and exporter with 554 employees in Henderson and Hopkins counties; and the Imperial Tobacco Company of Kentucky with 153 rehandlers. A warehouse of the American Snuff Company was located in Christian County, and Gallaher and Company, Limited, rehandled leaf in Webster and Henderson counties, to name a few. But the numbers were shrinking.

By 1929 the shape of the modern tobacco industry was beginning to jell: nationally, manufactures stood at $1.246 billion, about 85 percent of which was in cigars and cigarettes. Only about one-tenth the number of factories in 1904 were still in existence, and wage earners had dropped from a high of almost 179,000 in 1914 to a little over 116,000, although the value of manufactures was over five times that of 1899.[7] Thanks to Brown and Williamson and Axton-Fisher, Kentucky's production of cigars and cigarettes had tripled since 1927, though the sum was hardly more than a drop in the bucket to the national total; and North Carolina's leaf harvest of 454 million pounds for the first time exceeded Kentucky's 376.6 million. Burley was selling for about 20 cents a pound, and Western leaf at closer to 10 cents (see fig. 8); the last hogshead had been sold on an auction market.

But, of course, the Great Depression was at hand, with traumatic effects on the nation's entire economy. Nationally sales of all tobacco products dipped dramatically and did not regain their 1929 levels until 1937.

7. Except for a brief World War II surge, employment has continued to drop as automation and computerization have assumed an ever-larger role in production, until now there are 57,000 men and women working in leaf manufacturing, or half the 1929 total. At the same time, the value of tobacco products has increased by 500 percent, from $1.2 billion to $6.07 billion. Kentucky's labor force has remained virtually unchanged for years and now stands at about 15,000 (9,000 in manufacturing and 6,000 in rehandling operations).

Between 1929 and 1933 cigarette production dropped from over $436 million to little more than $281 million, cigars from about $280 million to $131 million, and chewing and smoking tobaccos from $145 million to $124 million. This sharp decline was inevitably reflected in leaf production and auction prices. In 1930 the 466,118 acres of Kentucky leaf yielded almost 377 million pounds, which brought but $64.25 million, or little better than 15 cents a pound for Burley, while Dark-fired prices dropped to 4 cents and in 1931 to 3 cents—a far cry from the 506 million pounds and $116 million of 1919. Crops the next three years brought between 8.6 cents (1931) and 12 cents (1932) for Burley; and after 1934, when the AAA began operations, acreages were reduced by a third or more, poundage averaged about a quarter-billion annually, and prices began edging up. As they did so later in the decade, production returned to the 350–400 million pound annual yields that had obtained earlier; but it was 1941 before dark leaf climbed back above 10 cents (see figs. 8 and 9).

Curiously, the Great Depression proved a benefit to Kentucky's incipient native tobacco manufacturing interests, although production and employment suffered at the local plants of American, Lorillard, Reynolds, and Liggett and Myers. These two small companies (by industry standards) were Axton-Fisher and Brown and Williamson; but by virtue of their smallness they had the flexibility required by the chaotic conditions in the marketplace for tobacco products to respond to opportunities quickly when they presented themselves and to capitalize on the marketing errors or complacency of the "Big Four." As it turned out, both conditions occurred simultaneously, and for a time in the early and middle 1930s these two relatively insignificant concerns enjoyed a spectacular jump in cigarette sales and production and threatened a serious challenge to the industry leaders, before they belatedly but successfully responded and eventually regained their domination of the market.

In order to tell this story, it is necessary to describe the history of these two companies, not only because they have come to dominate tobacco manufacturing in Kentucky and continue to do so, but also because they—or in the case of Axton-Fisher, its successor, Philip Morris—have made Louisville a powerful contender as a cigarette-making center with the established giants to the East—Raleigh-Durham, Winston-Salem, and Reidsville, North Carolina, and Richmond, Virginia. Indeed, between them they have restored Louisville to the prominence it last enjoyed as a manufacturing center when the National Tobacco Works was churning out sweet plug.

The Axton-Fisher Tobacco Company began modestly enough when, in the 1890s, a drummer for an Owensboro grocery house, Woodford F. Axton, started selling his own plug and twist to stores on his route. Trade grew, and eventually he brought his brother, Edwin D. Axton, into the operation to handle manufacturing and office operations, after which the company set up shop in Louisville and incorporated in 1904 with the name of George H. Fisher in the title (a fellow drummer and a remarkable poker player, Fisher put up a large part of the capital). Ten years later, business had so far expanded that a five-story factory and general office building was erected in Louisville, and a full line of tobacco products was made and distributed to an area that was expanding beyond the immediate region. Brands included "Clown" cigarettes; "Old Hillside," a bagged smoking tobacco; "Axton's Natural Leaf," a twist; and "White Mule," a plug.[8] Sales continued a spectacular

8. Axton-Fisher also made "Old Loyalty" and "Himyar" pipe mixtures and "Booster Twist," "8-Hour Union," "Pride of Dixie," and "Wage Scale" chewing tobaccos. As the names

climb. By 1922 Axton-Fisher's net worth was $667,000 on a balance sheet of $2.1 million. Sales hit $4.8 million by 1927, and in 1928 the company reorganized with capitalization of $4.5 million and entered into national competition in real earnest as one of the very few major independents. By 1933 demand for Axton-Fisher brands had so greatly increased that the plant and offices were doubled. Modern German-made cigarette machinery gave the plant a capacity of 24 million cigarettes a day. Completion of this expansion was timely, for Axton-Fisher had pioneered the development of the mentholated cigarette with "Spud," at 20 cents a pack (regular cigarettes sold at 15) in 1927, and for a "luxury" brand it was selling very well with annual sales of $5 million and profits of $500,000. Then, in June 1932, Axton-Fisher introduced "Twenty Grand," at 10 cents a pack, a full third cheaper than the 15 cent industry leaders, "Camel," "Lucky Strike," "Chesterfield," and "Old Gold"; and the low cost of this new brand had immediate appeal to a smoking public which was feeling the full rigors of the Depression. By September 1932 "Twenty Grand" was selling at an annual rate of 4.5 billion, or nearly 5 percent of the national total, and production limitations prevented the company from meeting more than 20 percent of its orders.

A year earlier, in June 1931, the "Big Four" had simultaneously announced an increase in the wholesale price of their cigarettes from $6.40 to $6.85 a thousand in a shortsighted and nearly disastrous attempt to restore falling profits, with the result that their sales fell by some 18 billion cigarettes that year. Into this vacuum

of these brands might suggest, Axton-Fisher management was in advance of its time in labor relations. It was the first major company to unionize its production workers, and it pioneered in other enlightened social programs for its employees, including free lunches.

leaped the ten-cent cigarette marketed by the smaller, more aggressive companies.[9]

The fact is that Axton-Fisher's "Twenty Grand" had been beaten into the marketplace by "Wings," a product of the brand-new Louisville tobacco company, Brown and Williamson, which had in 1927 become a subsidiary of the international leaf giant, the British-American Tobacco Company, Limited, and had the backing of the parent company's almost unlimited resources.[10] A much larger concern than Axton-Fisher, Brown and Williamson was better able to meet the unexpected demand for "Wings," and by the fall of 1932, helped along by a revival of the old coupon-redemption program, they were turning them out at an annual rate of 10.5 billion. Indeed, Brown and Williamson and Axton-Fisher between them captured fully 15 percent of the nation's cigarette sales, their production up from 2.7 billion cigarettes the first eight months of 1931 to 5.6 billion during a comparable period in 1932.

The challenge to the "Big Four" by the "ten-centers" was a short-lived phenomenon, however, for the industry leaders soon restored their earlier wholesale prices. Furthermore, the 10-cent cigarette was economically viable only as long as leaf prices were as depressed as they were during the bottom years of the Depression. In addition, profit margins on the

9. Actually, the first 10 cent cigarette on the market in any big way was Larus and Brothers' "White Rolls," in September, 1931, followed by Philip Morris's "Paul Jones" the next month.

10. The company began in Caswell County, North Carolina, as T. W. Williamson, a plug and smoakum manufacturer who, in the panic of 1893, merged with George T. Brown of Winston-Salem. Expansion brought such valuable brands as "Sir Walter Raleigh," which made the company attractive to British-American when they decided to penetrate the lucrative American market in 1927.

"ten-centers" were so narrow that provision for advertising costs could hardly be accommodated; and this was a fatal weakness in an industry in which the "Big Four" spent between $10 and $20 million a year for advertising—especially radio programs—during the 1930s. As leaf prices gradually rose after 1934 and the impact of mass-media advertising began to be felt, together with changes in corporate tax structure that penalized the smaller cigarette companies, the day of the ten-cent cigarette waned; and by the close of the decade the domination of "Camel," "Lucky Strike," and "Chesterfield" was as nearly complete as it had been in 1929. Still, by 1939 Brown and Williamson had secured 10.6 percent of the total, and Axton-Fisher 2.4 percent, down from the 1933–34 high of 4.4 percent.

Axton-Fisher management had clearly diagnosed the difficulties of their own and Brown and Williamson's situation; and early in 1936 they opened negotiations in London with British-American looking toward a merger of the two Louisville concerns into a single corporation with resources capable of doing battle with the "Big Four" on something like competitive equality. British-American executives, however, could not see the advantages of such an arrangement, at least on the terms offered by Axton-Fisher, and negotiations fell through. Still, it is interesting to speculate on the shape that might have been given to the tobacco industry in Kentucky and the nation had this merger of the two Louisville companies been consummated at that time.

Whatever that may have been, Axton-Fisher continued to search for a buyer and in 1941 found one in the Philip Morris Company, which was by then already so successful a merchandiser of cigarettes that it was desperately in need of expanded manufacturing capacity and reserves of leaf tobacco, both of which Axton-Fisher had in abundance. When the sale was effected, the last important tobacco company to be owned by native Kentuckians passed into the hands of a modern corporate structure, the ownership of which was elsewhere.

Nevertheless, the corporate history of Philip Morris is as interesting as that of Brown and Williamson or Axton-Fisher. Philip Morris began its existence as an individual, a London tobacconist dealing with the Victorian carriage trade, who capitalized on the new taste in hand-rolled Turkish cigarettes that Englishmen returning from the Crimean War (1854–1856) had brought with them as a gift from their allies, the Turks. These cigarettes, replete with cork tips and cotton filters, soon became fashionable in England and America, and by 1872 Philip Morris's agent in the United States enjoyed a lively snob trade in "Bond Street" and "English Oval" cigarettes, and later in another luxury brand, "Marlboro." Reincorporated as a Virginia firm in 1919 with American stockholders, Philip Morris did an increasingly successful cigarette business in "premium" brands, employing astute advertising and merchandising techniques and growing steadily in volume and sales the while, largely unnoticed by the rest of the trade.

In 1933, however, the company changed the play on its premium "Philip Morris" brand of cigarettes by reducing it to a popular 15 cent price, while advertising it as a "class" brand now available to the general smoker at a cost no greater than that of an ordinary cigarette. At the same time, it offered wholesalers and retailers a small break in their profit margins on the brand that encouraged them to push "Philip Morris" to their customers. Finally, they invested heavily in a clever advertising campaign featuring "Johnny," purportedly a bellhop in a fashionable hotel, and his cry, "Call for Philip Morris," and the brand caught on. Throughout the 1930s "Philip Morris" went in the face of industry trends by steadily increasing its sales, until by 1939 it had captured 7.1 percent of national cigarette sales.

Then in 1941, when a *Reader's Digest* survey of tar and nicotine content in cigarettes gave "Philip Morris" a decided edge over its rivals, a smoking public already nervous about the effect of nicotine addiction on health sent sales skyrocketing. At this point, Philip Morris bought out Axton-Fisher, which had lots of by-now unobtainable prewar tobacco and German-made cigarette machinery (World War II was already well advanced).

Thus in the generation following the dissolution of the Trust, the domination by cigarettes of American smoking preferences had become well established, as had the important place of White Burley leaf in their manufacture. Moreover, Kentucky's tobacco manufacturers had restored the state to some measure of the eminence it had enjoyed in the trade before the demise of chewing. Finally, intelligent cooperation between state and federal government and leaf growers was beginning to bring relative stability to the cultivation and marketing of leaf and a reasonable profit to planters. World War II was to work as profound a change on the tobacco industry as World War I had done; and the postwar years have brought Kentucky's leaf and leaf manufacturers to a leadership heretofore unprecedented.

7

Kentucky and Tobacco
Today, 1939–1974

A GLANCE at figure 7 will confirm that cigarette consumption jumped 75 percent between 1939 and 1945,
from 180 billion to 320 billion, largely attributable to
the wartime increase in women smokers, heavy shipments to the armed forces, and a sharp rise in teenaged
smokers, whom industry had been wooing for some
years. By 1954, when consumption nationally reached
400 billion, the first cigarette cancer scare coincided
with the introduction of the modern filtered cigarette. A
decade later a much more substantially documented
medical assault on the consumption of tobacco products,
founded upon their demonstrable tendency to induce a
variety of circulatory and respiratory ailments, further
disrupted the cigarette industry. Ironically, the chaos in
the marketplace that ensued worked to the enormous
benefit of Kentucky's leaf industry. During the same
period, a technological revolution in the state's tobacco
patches began raising production and prices together.

Thus while in 1947 the value of Kentucky's cigarette
production stood at $87 million out of a national total of
$1.1 billion, by 1954 the figure reached almost $328
million and four years later hit $430 million. Now at
over $700 million, manufacturers with plants in Ken-

tucky account for a third of the nearly 584 billion cigarettes annually produced in the United States, and 20 percent of the total is made in Louisville. Philip Morris and Brown and Williamson have wrested industry leadership from the "Big Four," and the value of the state's manufactured tobacco products now has reached about one billion dollars, second only to foodstuffs in our overall economy.

Kentucky's other tobacco manufactures should not be ignored. As of 1965, the Commonwealth (in this case Owensboro) turned out nearly 700 million cigars. The state also produced 15.5 million pounds of pipe tobacco and over 14 million pounds of scrap-chewing tobacco, as well as nearly a million pounds of other leaf products. Kentucky is the national leader in the manufacture of scrap-chewing tobacco with 43 percent of the total, and ranks third, behind Virginia and North Carolina, in pipe tobaccos with over a fifth of the total. The state's stemming, redrying, and rehandling industry has grown rapidly in the postwar years and now accounts for over $200 million annually. Huge warehouse complexes dotted around Lexington and the Bluegrass process and store White Burley leaf sold on the loose-leaf auctions in tens of thousands of hogsheads, where it is fermenting, aging, and mellowing under controlled temperature and moisture conditions during the two to three years required before it is ready for manufacture. Important rehandling centers are to be found in Northern and Western Kentucky as well, and loose-leaf auction sale of the state's various tobaccos constitutes an important industry in itself. Altogether, as of 1965 there were some thirty-seven tobacco manufacturers in Kentucky, of which half were in Louisville, employing about 9,000 workers; and twenty-six rehandling facilities gave jobs to another 6,000.

In figure 7 it can be seen that, in spite of soaring cigarette consumption in the United States since 1941 (sales have tripled), the regular-sized "Big Four" brands peaked out between 1945 and 1953, largely as a result of the rising popularity of the new king-sized cigarette pioneered by American's "Pall Mall" in 1939. The "Big-Four regulars" began their uninterrupted slide to their present insignificance in the market coincidentally with the development of the modern "filter" cigarette—actually, filters go back into the nineteenth century—and the enormous impetus given to their sales by the smoking-and-cancer scares of the mid-fifties and sixties. Brown and Williamson, which had pioneered the filter-tip field with its "Viceroy," introduced in 1936, also developed the first cellulose acetate filter for that brand in 1952 and within three years had captured over 60 percent of the nation's filter-tip business, although Lorillard's "Kent," with its "micronite" filter is generally given credit for the filter cigarette boom. In any event, Louisville profited from the filter-tipped cigarette craze, for both "Viceroy" and "Kent" were manufactured there. Furthermore, Philip Morris updated its "class" brands, "Marlboro," "Parliament," and "Benson and Hedges," and began to sell them at popular prices and in a growing variety of lengths and packages and filter tips, as did Brown and Williamson with "Raleigh."

Coincidental with all these changes in the cigarette industry in the last twenty years came an unaccountable increase in the demand for mentholated cigarettes. While this ultimate in tobacco adulterants was introduced by Axton-Fisher, it was Brown and Williamson's "Kool," first marketed in 1933, which cornered the mentholated cigarette market when the new surge to "cool" smoking hit late in the 1950s. With the addition of a filter tip, a profusion of mentholated brands emerged, including a new Brown and Williamson brand, "Belair."

What in essence has happened to the cigarette industry recently is that it has endlessly proliferated highly specialized brands, lengths, packaging gimmicks, filtration systems, and flavors, all of which have come more and more to be directed, not at a universal audience, but at specialized classes of smokers who are lured by advertising appeals calculated to foster a particular self-image, and whose fears about the cancerous effects of smoking are placated by filters and blends that claim to reduce tars and nicotine. Relatively small and flexible at the time when chaos hit the cigarette-buying public in the mid-1950s, and with none of the overwhelmingly dominant brands of older, regular cigarettes to make them complacent, Brown and Williamson, Philip Morris, and Lorillard have been far better able than their bigger competitors to adjust to a mass market of smokers with many different preferences in cigarettes. Thus Philip Morris, which markets "Marlboro" with an egregiously masculine appeal, offers that brand in fourteen different packages, lengths, and flavors (including a menthol)—all filtered, while "Benson and Hedges," which stresses still a luxury or class appeal (at a competitive price, of course) is offered in nine, including two "Deluxe" boxes, and "Virginia Slims" courts the liberated women smokers.

Furthermore, the smoking-and-cancer scare which hit the smoker also hit the manufacturers of tobacco products shortly thereafter, when overall consumption dropped briefly in 1964 (echoing the dip of 1955) and stimulated cigarette companies into a positive stampede to purchase concerns in other fields and with different product lines. At the head of the pack, which during the 1960s rushed to form what economists call "horizontal conglomerates," was Philip Morris; so that now, in addition to its tobacco interests, it is also involved internationally in a diverse range of products and activities, from chewing gum and razor blades to beer, packaging, printing, coatings, and land development.

If the progress in Kentucky's tobacco manufactures over the last generation has been spectacular, that in the cultivation of leaf has been no less so. A glance at figure 4 will show two surprising facts about the cultivation of tobacco in Kentucky: the first, that between 1866 and 1939 the average yield of leaf per acre, excluding annual variations, never exceeded 1,000 pounds, and usually ranged somewhere between 750 and 850 pounds; the second, that beginning in 1939 average leaf-production per acre embarked on a meteoric upward climb, until in 1969 it reached a peak of over 2,600 pounds, which was approached again in 1971. In other words, in the last thirty-five years, per-acre yield of Burley leaf has tripled.

Figure 3 demonstrates that Virginia and Tennessee production of leaf in total pounds, after a bulge in the 1940s and 1950s, has slipped back to about 100 million each, while that of North Carolina has continued the rapid rise begun in 1880 and accelerated after 1910 and again after 1935, and in the mid-1960s reached nearly 900 million pounds. Kentucky's production, meanwhile, has largely stabilized (as much as the unpredictability of growing conditions will allow) at between 350 and 500 million pounds, three times breaking the 500 million pound line established by the record-breaking 1919 crop, and once in the mid-1960s topping that mark.

These production records are all the more remarkable in the light of figure 4, which shows not only the decline of Dark-leaf production since the peak year of 1919 but also the equally sharp cut-back in Burley tobacco acres harvested since 1946, down from about 400,000 to the present total of about 150,000. Yet at the same time, on about one-third the total acreage, total pounds harvested equals or betters the production of the 1940s.

Figure 9 demonstrates a number of facts that bear on this discussion, not least of which is the rather chastening realization of how comparatively small the state's production of White Burley is—hardly more than about 20 percent of the total national production of all types of tobaccos, which reached the astonishing total in 1969 of over 2.3 billion pounds. But as figure 3 shows, of the great variety of leaf types and leaf tobacco growing regions which abound in the Southeastern United States, White Burley, and Kentucky, are only one.[1] Figure 11 also demonstrates that the increase in tobacco production nationally since 1941 has been accompanied by the same reduction in acreage as that in Kentucky; but most gratifying of all is the upward-sloping line marking the rising value of leaf crops to American farmers, which reached about $1.4 billion in 1969 on production of about 2.2 billion pounds, an average of nearly 70 cents a pound.

What has brought about this phenomenal improvement in the lot of the leaf planter in general, and of the Burley grower in particular, has been a remarkably successful partnership among all the parties interested in tobacco: the federal government, through the Department of Agriculture; the State Department of Agriculture; the School of Agriculture of the University of Kentucky; and the pools, namely, the Burley Tobacco Growers' Cooperative Association, the Eastern and Western Dark-fired, and the Stemming District Associations, in addition to the various warehouse associations and industries which serve the tobacco farmer.

Washington began it all in 1933 with the Agricultural Adjustment Act (AAA), which set up acreage restrictions on tobacco along with six other basic commodities and provided a government-supported loan program to farmers against surplus production. Following a further depression of the national economy and an adverse Supreme Court decision against the AAA, 1938 saw a reorganization of the Farm Price Stabilization Program. Marketing quotas based on acreage limitations (but not

1. The map reproduced in figure 5 does not include such important centers of leaf cultivation as Southeastern Pennsylvania, the Connecticut River Valley, Wisconsin, Minnesota, and Louisiana, the latter of which grows the remarkably rich, black "Perique" leaf, much prized by pipe smokers.

on production) were installed, subject however to an annual referendum among growers in which they ratified by a two-thirds vote or better the acreage allotments; and farmers who had not previously established a tobacco base (acreage) were discouraged from attempting to do so by a variety of penalties. Furthermore, the leaf marketing pools were put on a new and more commercially effective basis. Under the auspices of the federally financed Commodity Credit Corporation, leaf cooperatives were advanced capital and credit on an indefinite loan basis. This meant, first, that the grower got his money when his tobacco was sold, instead of having to wait for it until the cooperative had sold it, as before; and second, that the cooperative did not immediately have to sell surplus tobacco it had purchased. Reserves of leaf could be held in storage and advantageously disposed of later, during bad crop years, thereby stabilizing price and supply. By this time, furthermore, a complex system of typing and grading tobacco in all its various strains had been developed by federal and state marketing experts and enforced on the loose-leaf auction warehouse floor by government inspectors, who grade each basket of loose-leaf hands (bunches of leaves of the same grade tied together).[2] Concurrently, a system of price supports was developed by means of which leaf that did not bring the price thought appropriate for it was bought in by the government at 90 percent of that figure. This was called "parity" and was based on an indecipherable computation relating farm prices to a purchasing power constant. In effect, the government guaranteed that the price of leaf could not fall below a figure deemed equitable by Department of Agriculture statisticians. Needless to say, with booming demand for tobacco products at home and abroad, fixed tobacco acreage, and a floor supporting leaf auction prices, Burley could not help but increase

2. This was enacted into law by Congress in 1929.

in cost and hence in profitability to the by-now limited number of growers. The dream of the night riders had come true; there was a lock on the leaf market.

There was, however, a loophole built into the acreage-allotment and leaf price-support system. No limitation was placed on the total pounds of leaf a planter might be able to harvest and market from the acreage-base he was allowed by the latest referendum. Production therefore became an end to be sought as never before; and at this point the agriculture schools and the agri-chemical companies entered the leaf grower's life and work in a way he had never before experienced. The steep rise in the productivity of Burley leaf per acre, then, was no accident.

State land-grant colleges like the University of Kentucky had as one of their principal charges the improvement of the industrial and agricultural wealth of their people, and to rural Kentuckians better leaf production is an important ingredient in their well-being. Over the years, university scientists have contributed significantly to the development of improved hybrid strains of Burley which are more productive of leaf and more resistant to the countless diseases which plague this most delicate of plants. Research into methods of cultivation which, with augmented fertilizer applications, allowed planting seedlings much closer together in the field without significant loss of plant size and leaf production or quality, have been carried to local planters through the university's corps of county agents, with important improvements in poundage as the result. Scientific study of the causes and prevention of the diseases and pests which prey upon these succulent plants has resulted in the development of improved techniques in cultivation, curing and storing Burley leaf, and to the manufacture of a host of sprays, dusts, and other compounds which have proved helpful. Since the cultivation of tobacco, its curing and marketing, is one of the most demanding in terms of labor (it is estimated that between 280 and 350 man-hours are required to bring a single acre of leaf from plant-bed to market) and since rural Kentucky has been steadily depopulating, numerous labor-saving expedients have been devised to reduce the handwork formerly required for many operations in growing Burley. Pesticides have largely eliminated the hideous necessity of periodically picking off and mashing to death the huge green tobacco caterpillar which once so traumatized farm children of delicate sensibility. Herbicides have reduced weed control to manageable proportions, and fungicides have largely controlled the various rots to which tobacco is prone. Mechanization has facilitated planting considerably, but not harvesting (cutting), which remains a thoroughly miserable and time-consuming occupation, with "hanging" (putting the staked stalks up on barn rafters to cure) a close second. Finally, a great many products may be applied which discourage (but do not eliminate) the formation of "suckers," those secondary leaves which appear at the juncture of stalk and stem after the planthead, or blossom, has been "topped."

All these techniques, the result of elaborate research programs in state universities, in private industry, and in cooperative ventures, together with well-mounted informational and educational programs sponsored by federal and state agricultural departments and the Schools of Agriculture of such land grant institutions as the University of Kentucky, may be largely credited with the present superlative productivity of Kentucky's tobacco fields.[3]

Unfortunately, this application of science to leaf pro-

3. It is piquantly ironic, however, that equal credit for Kentucky's valuable Burley harvests should go to an engineer at the University of Louisville, Dean-Emeritus R. C. Ernst, who with the cooperation of Tennessee Eastman Company developed the modern cellulose-acetate cigarette filter in the early 1950s while a part-time research consultant with Brown and Williamson.

duction has not been without its unanticipated drawbacks to the tobacco industry as it is now constituted. Productivity ran so far ahead of acreage restrictions, for example, that by 1956 there were over 200 million pounds of leaf in storage in government-sponsored pools that had been bought up under the price-support program. With foreign buyers reducing their purchases and the legal limit on loans against leaf rapidly approaching, the support price on this unsalable tobacco was cut in half by the secretary of agriculture in an effort to encourage planters to reduce production of such decreasingly popular strains as Western Kentucky Dark leaf. As figure 4 shows, acreage allotments were sharply reduced after 1954's near-record Burley harvest and again after the all-time record crop of 1963; and comparable reductions in Western strains, already cut by falling demand, were also carried out. By the beginning of the 1970s a new program to limit overproduction was put into effect, and by means of a complicated formula both acreage planted and poundage produced were controlled, in the hope that exorbitant surpluses of leaf in pool storage could be reduced to manageable proportions.

The shoe, however, is rather on the other foot. Increased demand for Burley at home, where cigarette consumption rose by 4 percent in 1973 over the previous year to 584 billion, and abroad,[4] coupled with a succession of short crops in the 1970s, created a deficit of 360 million pounds of leaf that had to be covered by purchases from surpluses of earlier years stored in Pool warehouses. The result is that reserve supplies of Burley are nearly exhausted, and they were not replenished by price-support buying in the 1973 crop, for the already short supply of leaf and a lean harvest drove prices to an all-time high of over 93 cents a pound. Do-

4. 1973 U.S. exports of cigarettes jumped 20 percent, to 41.5 billion.

mestic and foreign demand for Burley would indicate a 1974 harvest of over 625 million pounds, but crop projections suggest that no more than 576 million pounds will actually cross the floors of the some 241 Burley auction warehouses now operating in the belt. U.S.D.A. officials are considering removal of acreage controls on Burley, Dark-fired, and Flue-cured leaf for the 1975 crop year.

The principal fear, of course, is that American Burley may price itself out of the market, as foreign and domestic buyers turn to cheaper, if inferior, leaf grown overseas, or worse yet, to synthetic tobacco compounds (i.e., pine wood pulp and other celluloselike material) currently being tested in some foreign countries. Exports of Kentucky leaf annually range between 60 and 70 million pounds, or about 15 percent of the state's crop; but exports are dropping, and the loss of these markets would deal a serious blow to planters. Furthermore, competition in the world leaf markets from African and Asian countries is increasing as quantity rises and quality improves. Rhodesia, for example, has been growing tobacco for some years now.

So far, the American cigarette industry has employed its technology successfully in devising ways of stretching its limited supplies of ever more costly domestic tobacco leaf. Called by the industry euphemism "extending" leaf's "filling characteristics," what this technology boils down to is a variety of ways of making the same amount of tobacco take up more space in a cigarette or pipe, chiefly through processes that involve freeze-drying or "puffing" leaf, or of salvaging parts of the tobacco plant that were thrown away in earlier times and reconstituting them into sheets, like paper, which can be employed in place of natural leaf. Nowadays, using these methods, only a little over two pounds of tobacco are required to make 1,000 cigarettes, whereas in 1960 manufacturing techniques demanded nearly three pounds. At some future time it may be possible to have a smoke that employs no tobacco at all!

The Burley industry is also threatened from other quarters as well. The very advances in agricultural technology that have recently produced leaf yields consistently over a ton an acre—high-yield strains, close planting, heavy fertilization, pesticides, fungicides, herbicides, and anti-sucker sprays—have also affected the quality of the leaf and its smoking properties, sometimes adversely. Fertilizers, for one, were found to alter the chemical composition, and particularly the all-important nicotine content, of tobacco leaf. But perhaps most serious of all has been the effect of the growth-inhibiting compounds used to control the formation of suckers by stopping the plant process called mitosis, or the division of new cells, while permitting the existing cellular structure of the leaves already sprouted to enlarge. Leaf growers took to this chemical at once, for it spared them the trouble of removing suckers by hand, as in the past, and it increased yield as well. Unfortunately, graders and buyers found that leaf so treated was often coarse, slick, and small, and not at all like the light, fluffy leaf that growers and agricultural scientists had spent so many years developing. This has, however, become an important area of research in plant chemistry and cultivation practices at the University of Kentucky and elsewhere. But meanwhile the severe manpower shortages in the Burley belt persist, limiting acreage and productivity, and little headway in mechanizing this largely hand-cultivated crop seems possible, at least to this observer.

The most serious long-term threat to the tobacco industry in recent years—although it has not had any apparent effect on cigarette sales except the popularity of the filter-tip—has come from the health sciences and their governmental agency, the Department of Health, Education, and Welfare, which have combined in an assault on smoking because of its statistically demonstrable role in the incidence of lung cancer, emphysema, heart and circulatory disease, and malfunctions of the nasal passages, sinuses, the mouth and throat, and the bronchial tubes, among a host of others. Nicotine, tars, resins, and other chemicals present in the smoke of tobacco have been experimentally shown to produce cancers in laboratory animals; and the constricting effect of nicotine on blood vessels, and many other deleterious physiological effects of smoking, are beyond serious question to any fair-minded person. In spite of this, spokesmen for the cigarette industry, with the arrogance and obtuseness for which tobacco makers have long been infamous, have either vehemently denied the allegations or more subtly attempted to confuse the issues. Opponents of smoking have nevertheless carried the day in the halls of Congress, where legislation prohibiting radio and television cigarette commercials has been enacted into law, as well as a requirement that each pack of cigarettes carry the following message: "Warning: The Surgeon General Has Determined That Cigarette Smoking Is Dangerous to Your Health."

Rather than fulminating against what everyone knows to be true,[5] the tobacco industry in Kentucky, together with state government, have taken a more enlightened

5. The toxic properties of N. tabacum were recognized, if not fully understood, as early as the sixteenth century, when for a time the plant was confused with the poisonous Henbane. Tobacco is now botanically grouped with the Nightshade family (Solanaceae), which carry the toxic alkaloids solanine (the various Nightshade varieties and the eyes and sprouts of the common Irish potato), hyoscamine (Henbane and Belladonna), and nicotine. Some members of this family, like Datura (jimsonweed), are hallucinogenic; and many of them, tobacco included, are psychoactive, that is, they affect the state of one's mind when used. This psychoactive effect is, of course, the principal appeal of tobacco to its users, and in nicotine is found the locus of its addictive properties.

approach to the problem of smoking and health and have created the Tobacco Research Board, which sponsors research at the University of Kentucky and elsewhere to explore the matter on a broad front. In part supported by a one-half cent state tax on cigarettes, federal funds, and grants from industry, researchers are looking for new leaf strains conspicuously low in nicotine and other possible cancer-causing agents and for new methods of cultivation and processing leaf that may fundamentally alter its characteristics, hopefully for the better. At the same time, basic research into the chemical composition of leaf itself, its possibly carcinogenic properties, and the activities of its various constituents when burned are among the topics under examination. But meanwhile, the consequences of the doctors' condemnation of tobacco may not begin to be felt for another generation.

Cigarette industry anxieties about the various threats to expanded tobacco addiction by the American public have issued in the formation over the years of a number of organizations dedicated to political lobbying in Congress and state capitals. The Tobacco Institute, the Tobacco Tax Council, and the Tobacco Growers' Information Committee, the latter of which has a state chapter and executive committee in Kentucky, are the most prominent and effective, recently combining to defeat a revenue measure in the 1972 session of the Kentucky General Assembly that would have raised the state tax on cigarettes from 3 to 5 cents a pack. Federal taxes on a pack of cigarettes amount to 8 cents, or about 56 percent of the package cost of 15 cents, and state and city taxes range from a low of 2 cents in North Carolina and 2.5 cents in Virginia to a high of 21 cents in Connecticut, 19 cents in New Jersey, and 18.5 cents in Texas, with New York, Minnesota, and Pennsylvania at 18 cents. Inevitably, there is a good deal of cigarette smuggling from low-tax states into high-tax states. Altogether, as of 1965, federal, state, and municipal authorities realized above $4 billion in revenue from tobacco products.[6] But the drying-up of other revenue sources for states and municipalities, together with the antitobacco crusade of health authorities, inevitably threaten tobacco with yet heavier levies.

One final anxiety hangs over the Burley belt, the threat of another antitrust suit against the major tobacco companies on the grounds of a conspiracy to fix Burley leaf prices, like the one launched against the American Tobacco Company and others in 1941, which resulted in a number of convictions and fines and was upheld by the Supreme Court in 1946, although follow-up action was not taken by any federal agency. The issue, which arose again during the unprecedentedly high-priced leaf auctions of 1973–1974, comes down to leaf growers' suspicions that, since almost all the leaf sold, no matter what its grade, went for approximately the same price, a conspiratorial system of allocations of leaf to buyers from different companies was in effect, even though the price was "top-dollar," and that in consequence the principle of a real auction had been subverted. The farmers were angered, suspecting that they had been done out of "dollar tobacco" by the city slickers from the big companies. The *Louisville Courier-Journal* ran an editorial on the subject (February 6, 1974), and the United States Department of Justice and a couple of congressional committees are "looking into the matter," as they say.

Suffice it to say, with tobacco in such short supply internationally in 1973–1974, all tobacco went for what the rival companies' bidders, on instructions from the home office, thought it would take to get an ample supply for future production, considering leaf inventories from earlier years and cost factors, both of which are likely to be very similar from company to company. In-

6. This figure has been kited by the Tobacco Tax Council, which includes sales taxes in their calculations.

deed, for a long time and largely out of fear of each other, the major tobacco companies' buyers have adhered rather closely to each other's price lines in tobacco auctions, if only in order to maintain an orderly market and to prevent a rival from gaining a competitive advantage; and the price-support and acreage-allocation programs of the government have only encouraged this trend.[7] The question of "conspiracy in restraint of trade" on which an antitrust action hinges rests finally on what one means by "conspiracy." In this case, a deliberate plot to hold down prices hardly seems justified by the exceedingly complicated economics of the tobacco industry. What appears to be the case, as it has been for a long time now, is a general industry recognition that, Burley leaf marketing conditions being what they are, a policy of protective parity in the cost of tobacco to them in any given year is as necessary as a rough equivalence in the price of their finished products, profit margins across the industry being as exquisitely narrow as they are. Competitive warfare is thus confined to the relatively bloodless fields of advertising and merchandising.

But it is questionable how many people in and out of the industry, government, and agriculture accept the views outlined above; and this being Kentucky, there will no doubt be no small modicum of moving and shaking in all branches of the leaf economy during the bicentennial year and beyond. Indeed, on July 31, 1974, a class-action suit for damages of $3 billion was filed against the major tobacco companies by a half-dozen Kentucky planters, charging price-fixing in auction sales.

7. Forty years ago, when that devoutly maverick independent, my father, was with Axton-Fisher, his leaf buyers were instructed to follow the price line per grade bid at auction by American buyers, "because they are the best judges of leaf." What my father meant was that tobacco bought at these prices would keep his firm's costs competitive.

Epilogue

THE STORY of Kentucky and its tobacco has brought us a long way from that day now lost in the mists of prehistory when some inquisitive Algonkin first discovered the heady pleasures of nicotine and passed the secret on to his people. From that problematical time until now, the trail of tobacco has taken us round the world and down through some ten or twelve millennia to the founding of our Commonwealth, and thence to the present day.

Through it all, our story has touched in one way or another on almost every aspect of human endeavor: war and insurrection, medicine, economics, politics, agriculture, revolution, government, even education and religion, for tobacco has from the first been intimately involved with the human being in almost all his aspects, used, abused, exploited, damned, and idolized.

Closer to home, the successive strains of Burley have brought prosperity and ruin, serenity and violence, prestige and obscurity to Kentucky's planters, merchants, and manufacturers, and through it all, have provided revenue to the government. Kentuckians and their prize leaf have been helped or hurt by a succession of revolutions in government, industry, genetics, agriculture, commerce, and automation. What lies ahead for the state's principal cash farm crop and major industry is anybody's guess, but it is safe to say that our fellow citizens will not take it lying down. There are more things than politics that are the "damnedest" in Kentucky.

Figure One

1850 Tobacco Production in Kentucky

Figure Two

Tobacco Producing Areas (S.E.)

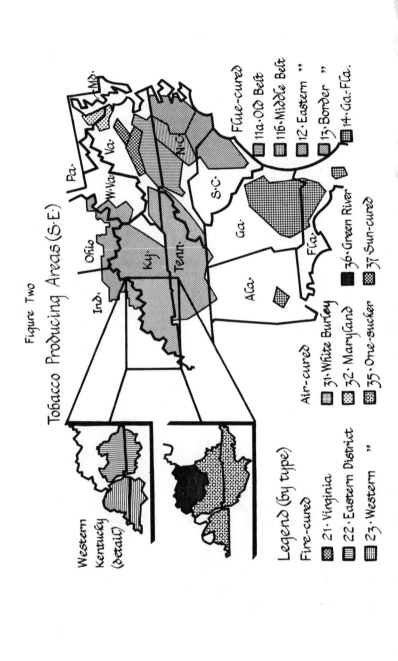

Western Kentucky (detail)

Legend (by type)

Fire-cured
■ 21 · Virginia
▨ 22 · Eastern District
▤ 23 · Western ''

Air-cured
▨ 31 · White Burley
▦ 32 · Maryland
▨ 35 · One-sucker
■ 36 · Green River
▨ 37 · Sun-cured

Flue-cured
▨ 11a · Old Belt
▤ 11b · Middle Belt
▨ 12 · Eastern ''
▨ 13 · Border ''
▨ 14 · Ga.-Fla.

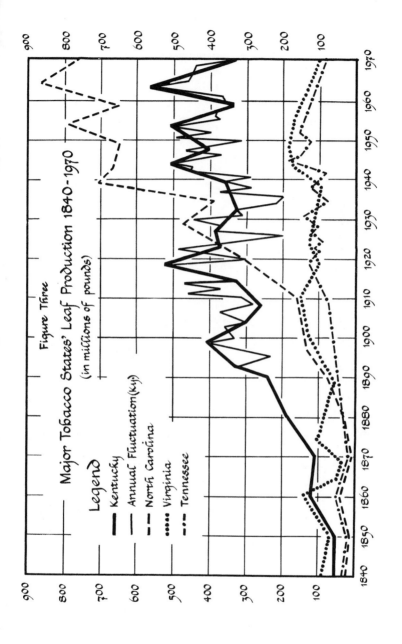

Figure Three

Major Tobacco States' Leaf Production 1840-1970

(in millions of pounds)

Legend
Kentucky
Annual Fluctuation (Ky.)
North Carolina
Virginia
Tennessee

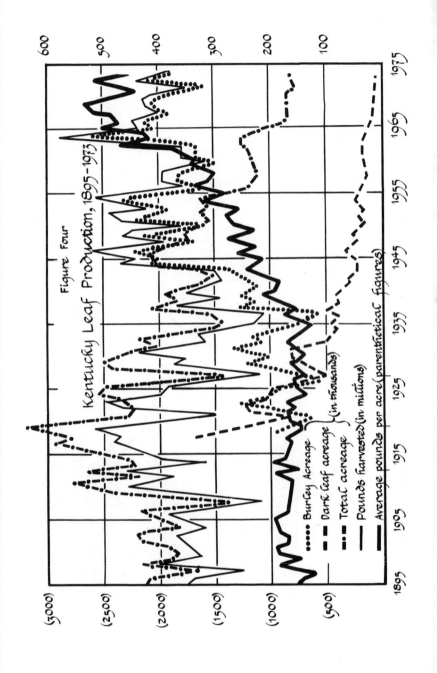

Figure Four

Kentucky Leaf Production, 1895-1973

······· Burley Acreage
------- Dark Leaf acreage } (in thousands)
-··-··- Total acreage
——— Pounds harvested (in millions)
——— Average pounds per acre (parenthetical figures)

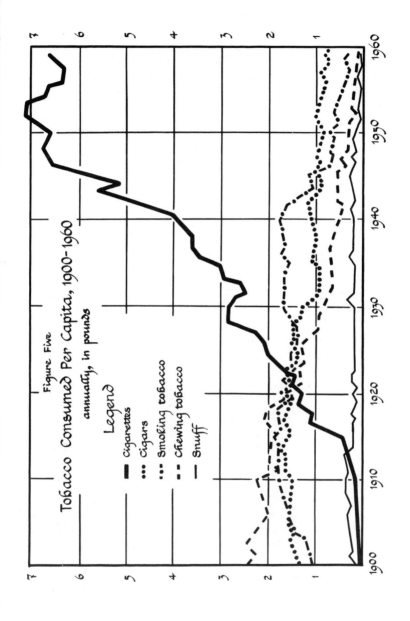

Figure Five

Tobacco Consumed Per Capita, 1900–1960

annually, in pounds

Legend

Cigarettes

Cigars

Smoking tobacco

Chewing tobacco

Snuff

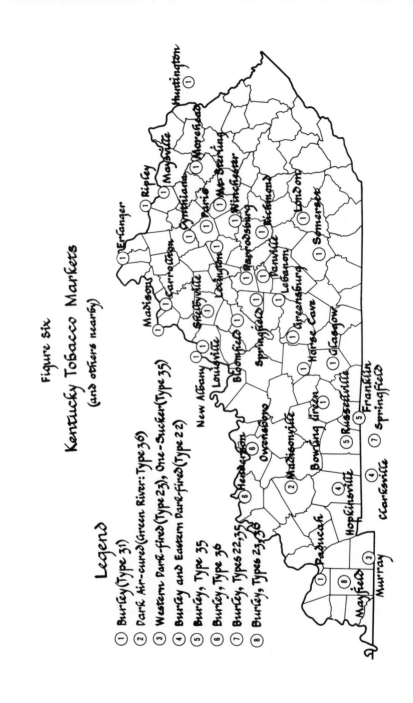

Figure Six

Kentucky Tobacco Markets
(and others nearby)

Legend

① Burley (Type 31)
② Dark Air-cured (Green River: Type 36)
③ Western Dark-fired (Type 23), One-Sucker (Type 35)
④ Burley and Eastern Dark-fired (Type 22)
⑤ Burley, Type 35
⑥ Burley, Type 36
⑦ Burley, Types 22, 35
⑧ Burley, Types 23, 36

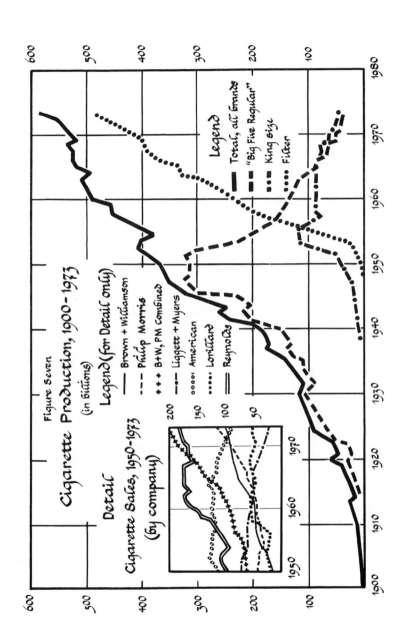

Figure Seven

Cigarette Production, 1900–1973
(in billions)

Legend (for Detail only)
——— Brown + Williamson
– – – Philip Morris
+++ B+W, PM Combined
–·–· Liggett + Myers
ooooo American
····· Lorillard
═══ Reynolds

Legend
▬▬ Total, all brands
– – – "Big Five Regular"
······ King size
▬ ▬ Filter

Detail
Cigarette Sales, 1950–1973
(by company)

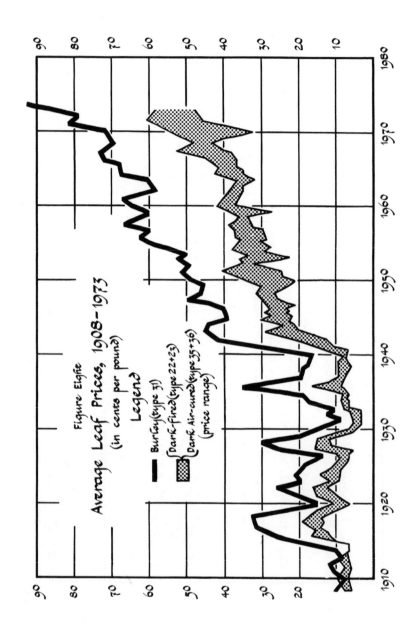

Figure Eight

Average Leaf Prices, 1908–1973
(in cents per pound)

Legend

■ Burley (type 31)
▧ { Dark-Fired (type 22+23)
▧ { Dark Air-cured (type 35+36)
(price range)

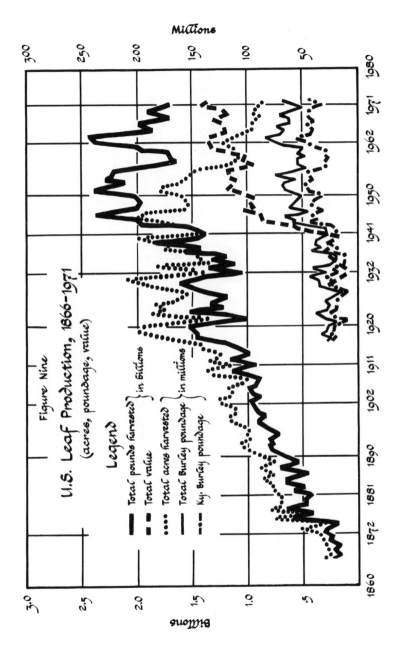

Figure Nine

U.S. Leaf Production, 1866–1971
(acres, poundage, value)

Legend

Total pounds harvested } in billions
Total value
Total acres harvested } in millions
Total Burley poundage } in millions
Ky. Burley poundage

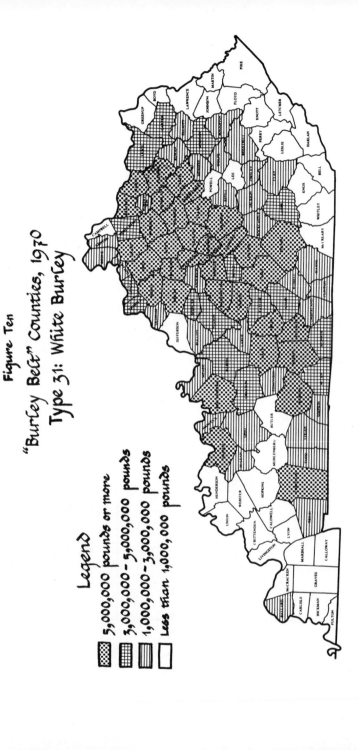

Figure Ten

"Burley Belt" Counties, 1970

Type 31: White Burley

Legend

5,000,000 pounds or more

3,000,000 - 5,000,000 pounds

1,000,000 - 3,000,000 pounds

Less than 1,000,000 pounds

Figure Eleven

Dark-fired Tobacco Growing Counties, 1970
Types 22 and 23: East and West Fire-cured

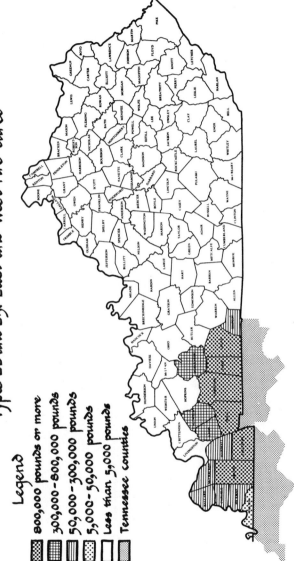

Legend

800,000 pounds or more
300,000 - 800,000 pounds
50,000 - 300,000 pounds
5,000 - 50,000 pounds
Less than 5,000 pounds
Tennessee counties

Figure Twelve

Dark Air-cured Tobacco Growing Counties, 1970

Types 35 and 36: One-Sucker and Green River

Legend

700,000 pounds or more

200,000–700,000 pounds

50,000–200,000 pounds

5,000–50,000 pounds

Less than 5,000 pounds

Tennessee counties

Bibliographical Note

General Histories. Robert K. Heimann, *Tobacco and Americans* (1960) is probably the best all-round study, but see also Jerome E. Brooks, *The Mighty Leaf* (1952) and J. C. Robert, *The Story of Tobacco in America* (1949). The latter has an excellent bibliography.

Early Histories. Jerome E. Brooks, *Tobacco: Its History Illustrated by the Books, Manuscripts, and Engravings in the Library of George Arents, Jr.,* 4 vols. (1937–1943) is an annotated bibliography of the Arents Collection in the New York Public Library, the largest such collection in the world. Other important holdings are in the Duke University Library and the Tobacco Museum, Danville, Virginia. Sarah A. Dickson, *Panacea or Precious Bane: Tobacco in Sixteenth-Century Literature* (1954) is also from the Arents Collection, as is Herbert J. Spinden, *Tobacco Is American: The Story of Tobacco before the Coming of the White Man* (1951). A mine of information on the early cultivation of leaf is G. Melvin Herndon, ed., *William Tatham and the Culture of Tobacco* (1969), a reprint of Tatham's *An Historical and Practical Essay on the Culture and Commerce of Tobacco* (1800). C. M. MacInnes, *The Early English Tobacco Trade* (1926) is authoritative. Anthropological studies include Peter Farb, *Man's Rise to Civilization* (1968); W. D. Funkhouser and W. S. Webb, *Ancient Life in Kentucky* (1928); *Tobacco and Smoking in Art* (1960); George A. West, *Tobacco, Pipes, and Smoking Customs of the American Indians* (1934: repr. 1970); Clark Wissler, *Indians of the United States* (1971); and Douglas W. Schwartz, *Conceptions of Kentucky Prehistory* (1967).

Regional Histories. The standard work remains Thomas D. Clark, *A History of Kentucky,* rev. ed. (1960), but see also Lewis Collins, ed., *Collins' History of Kentucky,* 2 vols., rev. ed. (1874); W. E. Connelley and E. M. Coulter, *Kerr's History of Kentucky,* 5 vols. (1922); Humphrey Marshall, *A History of Kentucky* (1824). Specialized studies include Maury Klein, *History of the Louisville and Nashville Railroad* (1972), Mary Verhoeff, *The Kentucky River Navigation* (1917), and Benjamin Casseday, *History of Louisville* (1852).

Studies of the Tobacco Industry. On manufactures, see V. S. Collins, *History of Manufactures in the United States, 1607–1928,* 3 vols. (1929); Reavis Cox, *Competition in the American Tobacco Industry, 1911–1932* (1933: repr. 1968); Meyer Jacobstein, *The Tobacco Industry in the United States* (1907: repr. 1968); R. B. Tennant, *The Rise of the Cigarette Industry* (1950); and John K. Winkler, *Tobacco Tycoon: J. B. Duke* (1942). More generally, see L. C. Gray, *History of Agriculture in the Southern United States to 1860* (1949) and A. P. Whitaker, *The Spanish-American Frontier* (1927).

Specialized Studies. On the health consequences of tobacco use, a number of studies may be had from the National Clearinghouse for Smoking and Health, U.S. Department of Health, Education, and Welfare, including: *The Health Consequences of Smoking* (1973), *Tobacco Smoking Patterns in the United States, 1880–1965* (1965), and *The Use of Tobacco: Practices, Attitudes, Knowledge, and Beliefs* (1972).

On tobacco as a psychoactive drug, see Efron, Holmstedt, and Kline, *Ethnopharmacologic Search for Psychoactive Drugs,* U.S.P.H.S. Bulletin no. 1645 (1967); R. E. Schultes and A. Hoffmann, *The Botany and Chemistry of Hallucinogens* (1973); and Tony Swain, ed., *Plants in the Development of Modern Medicine* (1972).

On the Black Patch War, the standard work is James O. Nall, *The Tobacco Night Riders of Kentucky and*

Tennessee (1939), but see also H. H. Kroll, *Riders in the Night* (1965), John G. Miller, *The Black Patch War* (1936); and Robert Penn Warren's novel *Night Rider* (1939).

Others. The only extant account of the history of tobacco in Kentucky is a pamphlet issued by the Tobacco Institute, *Kentucky and Tobacco*, 4th ed. (1972). Another pamphlet published by the American Tobacco Company has a self-explanatory title: *Burley Tobacco: Diseases, Nutrient Deficiencies and Excesses, Injuries, Pests, Cured Tobacco* (1958). Among special studies see D. G. Card, "The Market Price of Burley Tobacco" (Ph.D. diss., Cornell University, 1939); H. B. Clark, The Role of Farmers' Cooperative Associations in the Marketing of Dark Tobacco in Kentucky and Tennessee, 1931–1950 (Ph.D. diss., University of Kentucky, 1950); and T. F. Johnson, Cigarette Tobacco Production and Prices (Ph.D. diss., University of Virginia, 1949). See also the series of *Fortune Magazine* articles on the cigarette industry in the 1930s: "One out of Every Five Cigarettes," 6:44ff.; "Spuds," 6:50ff.; "Philip Morris and Co.," 13:106ff.; and "The Old Gold Contest," 16:49ff.

Original sources of information include the Agricultural Experiment Station, University of Kentucky, which issues annual statistical bulletins on agricultural production as well as periodic compilations, notably the following: D. G. Card and James Koepper, *Prices of Products Bought and Sold by Kentucky Farmers, 1909–1952*, Bulletin no. 601 (1953), and Bulletin no. 710, for the years 1950–1968 (1970). The University of Kentucky Cooperative Extension Service distributes pamphlets on a variety of tobacco-related subjects; note particularly Ira E. Massie et al., *Tobacco Production in Kentucky*, Circular 482-B (1971); *Harvesting and Curing Burley Tobacco*, Circular 600 (n.d.); and *Preparing Burley Tobacco for Market*, Circular 579-A (n.d.).

The "Annual Report on Tobacco Statistics" is published each spring by the Tobacco Division of the Agricultural Marketing Service, United States Department of Agriculture, Washington, D.C., with separate sections for Burley and Dark-leaf. They also issue a quarterly, "The Tobacco Situation," and periodically publish a statistical compendium of leaf production. Exports are included in the "Annual Report." The U.S.D.A. Bureau of Agricultural Economics in 1948 published *Tobaccos of the United States: Acreage, Yield per Acre, Production, Price, and Value: by States, 1866–1945 and by Types and Classes, 1919–1945*. The U.S.D.A. Agricultural Marketing Service also issued *Tobacco in the United States: Production, Marketing, Manufacturing, Reports*, Misc. Pub. no. 867 (1973).

The Kentucky Department of Agriculture, Crop and Livestock Reporting Service also publishes each spring the *Kentucky Agricultural Statistics* for the previous year. In 1966 the Division of Markets, Kentucky Department of Agriculture, issued *Kentucky Agricultural Statistics: Centennial Issue (1866–1965)*, a valuable compilation. See also E. F. Seiller, *Kentucky Resources and Industries*, Kentucky Bureau of Agriculture, Labor, and Statistics, Bulletin 34 (1926): *Progress Report*, Kentucky State Planning Board, rev. ed. (1935); and Jess B. Thomas, *Tobacco Marketing Practices in Kentucky*, Legislative Research Commission Report 31 (1965).

The Bureau of Alcohol, Tobacco, and Firearms, Internal Revenue Service, U.S. Treasury Department, publishes annual résumés of taxes collected on tobacco products which provide an index of production; but the simplest expedient is the annual summary of cigarette sales by company and brand to be found (since 1941) in *Printer's Ink*, the trade magazine of the advertising industry. See also the trade magazine, *Tobacco*. Finally, the Tobacco Tax Council periodically issues *The Tax Burden on Tobacco, Historical Compilation*, the latest of which (vol. 8) appeared in 1973.

A special item is valuable: *Report of Burley Auction*

Sales, 1916–1968, Carrollton Redrying Company, Carrollton, Kentucky, 1969.

Various tobacco industry trade organizations publish special-interest materials which may be had for the asking: Tobacco Growers' Information Committee, Inc., Box 12046, Cameron Village Station, Raleigh, N.C. 27605; The Tobacco Institute, 1735 K. Street N.W., Washington, D.C. 20006; and the Tobacco Tax Council, Inc., Box 8269, Richmond, Va. 23226.

Tubular Pipe

Ovoid Pipes

Bird Totem Pipe

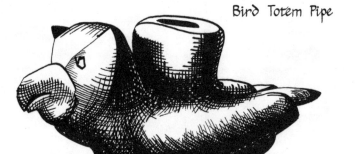

Double Conoidal Pipe

Micmac Pipe